Why Write Letters

SCHAPER

DONNA E.

Why Write Letters
10 Ways to Simplify —
and Enjoy — Your Life

the pilgrim press   cleveland, ohio

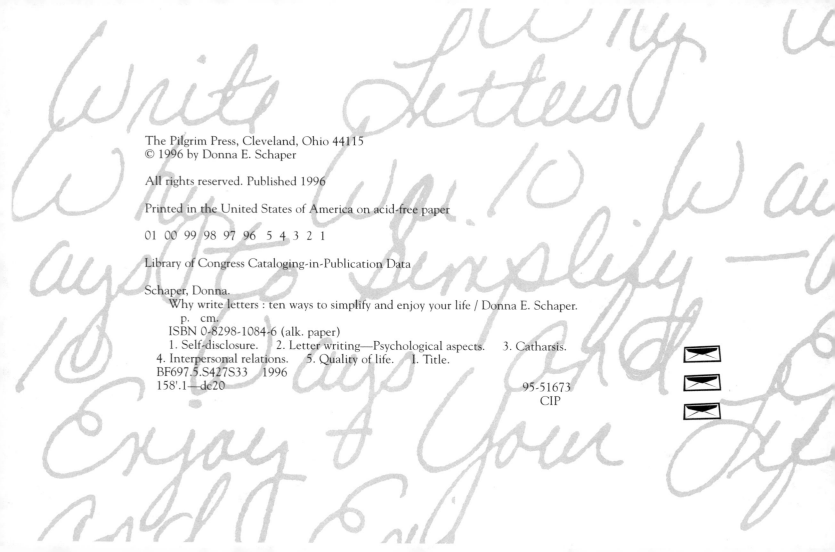

The Pilgrim Press, Cleveland, Ohio 44115
© 1996 by Donna E. Schaper

Printed in the United States of America on acid-free paper

01 00 99 98 97 96   5 4 3 2 1

Library of Congress Cataloging-in-Publication Data

Schaper, Donna.
    Why write letters : ten ways to simplify and enjoy your life / Donna E. Schaper.
      p.   cm.
    ISBN 0-8298-1084-6 (alk. paper)
    1. Self-disclosure.   2. Letter writing—Psychological aspects.   3. Catharsis.
    4. Interpersonal relations.   5. Quality of life.   I. Title.
BF697.5.S427S33   1996
158'.1—dc20
                                                    95-51673
                                                    CIP

contents

Write Letters Why
Why Wait. W
ays to Simplify —
10 Ways and
Enjoy your Lif

why

WHY WRITE LETTERS IS A STRATEGY FOR LIVING SIMPLY IN A COMPLICATED WORLD. AS STRATEGY, IT IS BOTH A REAL AND A SYMBOLIC PATTERN. WRITING LETTERS, GROWING LETTUCE, AND RIDING TRAINS ARE ALL LOW-COST FORMS OF PERSONAL ENTERTAINMENT; THEY ARE ALSO WAYS WE CAN COMBINE WORK AND PLAY, WHICH IS HUMAN BEING AND HUMAN DOING AT THEIR BEST. SUCH ACTIVITIES REMIND US WHO WE WANT TO BE.

They are also forms of resistance to the way culture and economy, as currently constituted, want us to live. They slow down fast life. They are low-tech in a high-tech world. Not so grand as a vision or blueprint for the "new" world, or even rules for living simply in complex times, the activities I discuss in this book are a few small, and possibly effective, first steps toward a refreshed life.

Why do we fail to write the letters we could, all the while wringing our hands in artificial powerlessness? Why do we buy macaroni and cheese in tin pans for $4.95—enough, purportedly, to feed a family—when we could make the same thing in our own (grandmother's) casserole dish for a lot less and have it taste twice as good? Many people say they "don't have the time." I say we have the time but not the will.

Why Write Letters is also a strategy for reading our own experience, for looking deeply enough to see what we really want. It is spiritual judo: we toss *slow* back at *fast*. We toss *less* back at *more*. We toss *quality* back at *quantity*. We make a slight move and have a grand effect.

Why Write Letters is like a child's picture book: it shows the way. When we use a library instead of a bookstore or take a train instead of a plane, we act parabolically on behalf of the life we want. The book is for those of us who fear that our lives are being run by someone, or some things, besides ourselves. It has a spirituality (the name of the Spirit by which it lives) and a theology (its best view of God) implicit in itself.

Judith Plaskow, the Jewish feminist, explains the strategy well. She goes a step beyond the feminist slogan about the political being the personal and vice versa. She says we now know that "the spiritual is political. Our difficulties in projecting our spiritual futures were likewise connected to larger structural issues. . . . In this situation, politics, we realized, is the necessary work we do to make the world safe for our spirituality."[1] I propose herein that we use the political to make our spiritual selves safe also. We don't stay away from the political nor do we stop there. The point is a *life*, not *politics*. The point is living, not just changing the world so we can live.

Many of us know the critical nature of the task of changing the world to make it safe for human beings, as children and as adults. We know that the world's values are less than fully human. *Fast, more,* and *most* do not make us well. The technologically based global economy, here and coming, carries values in its suitcase and in its fiber optics. The economic pattern may differ from that of the Industrial Age but the values have not shifted—yet. These values are efficiency, productivity, and growth. They are in charge of the ways we make our living. When I speak of being counterculture, I also mean making a small space in our days when we are countering economy as well as culture. How? By living differently.

Often when we write a letter to a trusted friend, we find out what we really think about what is going on in our lives. We discover whose values govern us. We find out what values we are living by—and we articulate those we prefer.

If Antonio Gramsci had failed to write his *Letters from Prison*, we might not know of his grand effort to pry communism open in Italy as it turned Fascist. Because he bothered to write letters, we know his companionship in our own struggle against rulers we did not choose. We know that he was a "pessimist of the intellect and an optimist of the will" because he took the time to tell us in a way that could be heard.

Anne Morrow Lindbergh, a co-pilot and mother of five, wrote enough letters for an editor to collect. In them, we discover that she spent more than one night enjoying an Iowa dusk. That recorded enjoyment spurs us on to living more in our own moments and our own dusks. We think of all the awe in her life and are glad to know that she found a way to record some of it. There may already be more awe in our lives than we know. We may just not have taken the time to see it.

Both columnist Ellen Goodman and Vivian Gornick plead with the public to write letters.[2] Their plea is about the values of *slow* and *small* and the need to record how much each matters to each of us, in different and particular ways.

This book joins their plea. It foments revolt against the values of *fast, more,* and *big.* These patterns have begun to damage many of us. In response, we can instead do what most powerless people have done throughout the centuries. With the slaves, we can sing a song the master can't understand. We can live by the beat of a drum the status quo can't quite hear. With our marching orders of fast, more, and most blaring in our ears, we can go slow, care well for a little, live by and with less. We can do simple things that say we are not with the current but against it. Even if the current can't hear us, we can

hear ourselves. I think of members of the Pentecostal church in Chile moving through their government building singing their favorite song, "Deo Gracias." As they move through the building, they shift the words to "Democracias." The authorities mishear the words. The church people continue to sing. (This report from our Massachusetts delegate to Chile in 1994 taught them all a lot: just changing the words of a song can be a radical act.)

Even, and especially, if the things we do are ridiculously small, we do them as a defense of our spirits. Spiritual judo is the strategy we use; we have no army or alternative economy. Culture wants *speed;* we can crawl. They want action *now;* we can procrastinate. They want *efficiency;* we can do each step twice. They want *disposability;* we can endure. They want us to *buy* tapes and videos and books—including this one; we will borrow them. They want the domestic arts to disappear; we will employ them. We will use our own macaroni-and-cheese recipe instead of their box or their pan.

We may not be able to use our judo at work and still be employed, but we can use it in our homes. Some of us can live well in both places but, prior to economic revolution in the workplace, that will remain a minority. Instead, we can do what the Eastern Europeans did as communism fell: we can learn to play cards very, very well, and wait. Playing cards is what Adam Michnik, the great Polish organizer and writer, recommended as political strategy as communism was overthrown in Poland. He understood the powerlessness of the people, but he also understood they had places, like their homes and neighborhoods, where they could still exercise power on their own behalf.

The "whys" in this book are invitations to power. They go from very small things to very large things on purpose: small is what matters, not large. They make the argument of why we should treasure, value, and use the small. They try to be less "anti-large" than "pro-small."

David Frost tells a story of traveling to an interior African country. Question six on the passport form was, "Is overthrowing the government the reason you are here?" Frost swears he wrote on the form, "Not sole purpose of visit." Those of us who want to live as our own personal property don't have the time to overthrow the culture; we just want to assure ourselves of our own time and space within it. We are quietly subversive.

This quiet subversiveness is particularly critical in an area most of us care deeply about: the raising of our children. We live with enormous tension in raising our children to fit into a world many of us don't like very much. But if we raise our children in the calm of *slow* rather than the anxiety of hurry, we can

raise them close enough to the system to keep them safe and far enough away to keep them even safer. The paradox is important.

There is tremendous complexity in raising children calmly and courageously, with and in the system rather than too far outside. *Why Write Letters*, while it offers a strategic way to raise children, is not fundamentalist or perfect parenting! Rather, it is parenting by accompaniment, by slow travel along the dangerous road that is modern culture. It is showing, not telling the children, that we live by a different drummer.

Domestic life is still a place where some of us can find spiritual sustenance—and where children are counting on it. We hear the common remark, "My house is a mess." People aren't kidding. *Why Write Letters* is a strategy to restore permission for the domestic arts; it is also a call to feminists to look more deeply into why we have abandoned the domestic arts. The answer is embarrassing: we sang the master's songs, wore his suits, kept his hours, thought his thoughts—and still only made fifty-three cents on his dollar. That situation is improving but nowhere near equality yet.

If we can make time in our days and weeks to enjoy the simple things—write letters, grow lettuce, unlock doors, sing songs, keep house, spend more time at home, use the branch library, take trains, use calm as well as courage, keep Sabbath—there might even be time to supervise children and their TV screens, or get them off their screens with a little more frequency. We may just find that the simple pleasures of the smaller steps open up space for the larger changes to emerge. Such changes emerge when we accept the invitation to write letters; and we may find that we like writing letters very much.

Sappho, the Greek poet, dared us to just this strategy of emergence when she said, "Find peace in yourself; then others will follow you anywhere." Why write letters? To find peace. Calm. Fun. Serenity. When we take back our peace, we have written a long and beautiful letter to ourselves.

N o t e s

1. Judith Plaskow, "Spirituality and Politics: Lessons from B'not Esh," *Tikkun* (May/June 1995): 31.

2. Ellen Goodman, syndicated column in *New York Times*, 7 July 1994; and Vivian Gornick, "Letters Are an Act of Faith: Telephone Calls Are a Reflex," *New York Times Book Review*, 31 July 1994, 4.

Write Letters Why u

Why Wait Wa

ays to Simplify —

10 Ways and

Enjoy † Your Lif

Chapter 1
why write letters

WRITING LETTERS IS A SIMPLE FORM OF OBEDIENCE TO THE GOLDEN RULE. IT DOES TO OTHERS WHAT WE WOULD LIKE THEM TO DO TO US. FINDING A PIECE OF REAL MAIL IN THE MAILBOX IS SUCH A CAUSE FOR JOY THAT WE SHOULD ALL BE SPENDING A FEW MORE DIMES PER DAY ON IT. IF YOU DON'T SEND LETTERS, YOU WON'T GET LETTERS. YOU MAY NOT EVEN GET THEM IF YOU DO SEND THEM, BUT AT LEAST IN SENDING THEM YOU SET UP THE POSSIBILITY OF GIFT.

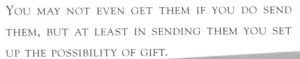

My friend insisted she didn't have time to write letters—so I sent her a package of postcards. Use them, I said. Why write letters or postcards? To connect. To greet. To disclose. To find out what we are really thinking. Letters and cards take so little money to mail that we can hardly think we are paying for them.

Writing letters encourages self-expression. It tells us what we are thinking. We may not have taken the time lately to find out!

Writing letters causes our ears to begin to work in a sense. We listen in on the other person's house, no matter how far away, and try to remember what we know about their stage of existence. How is her cancer developing? Is it still of remission? Did the tomatoes grow this year or not? What happened to the daughter who had twins? Did the congregation fire the old pastor? In remembering what we know of other people's lives, we broaden the data of our own days, the matter in our own minds. We relax in other people's trouble and give our own a break.

Writing letters does not have to be profound. We don't need to rise that far above small talk for the letter to work. In fact, the closer we stay to what happened today, the better. What did the dawn look like? Who had what for breakfast? Who is in a bad mood? Who called before 8 A.M.? Did you wear the scarf she gave you? Why? Why not? How did you travel to work and what happened on the way? Are you still getting bagels at the same place? What about the new gourmet coffee? How much do you hate—or love—your boss? Has that changed? Did you walk at lunch or read?

Is there time for prayer in your day? If so, how? How can you inquire as to the status of prayer in your correspondent's life without guilt being the legacy of the inquiry? Work at it. (The trick is mutual vulnerability, not sending your vulnerability in the mail.)

What are you looking forward to? What about the season or its smells? Where were you last year at this time? When will you and your correspondent visit again?

In a recent writing seminar at Kirkridge, a popular Protestant retreat center in Pennsylvania, a woman wrote the story of a close friend visiting after a long absence. She described the relationship as one that was life-changing when it was young, and now "just Christmas cards, not even a note." We all knew exactly what she meant.

Another participant in the workshop talked about yelling at her son at the end of a weekend visit from college, "just because he picked up two mugs in the sink and began to wash them." At first no one understood. Then she explained: The washing of the mugs meant the visit was over; she had wanted it to linger a little longer.

Wouldn't that scene in the kitchen make a good letter to a friend long absent? It might even reignite the relationship. Writing letters has other advantages besides maintaining friendships. It also causes a human record to develop. It gives us something with which to entertain our grandchildren—they will read our letters, but not our electronic mail. (They could read our e-mail, of course, but we would have to value what we said there enough to preserve it for posterity.) We will want our heirs to know just how strange we were. It will help them develop an appropriate life perspective—and not be so concerned about how strange they are.

I remember once a correspondence I had with a friend in Alaska. She was a United Methodist clergywoman who did not know that when she became pastor in Nome, she would also become the morti-cian. She had to learn embalming right away—and did. Having to learn so intimately about death became such a strain on her that, when added to the sunless days, she became quite depressed. She wrote about the depression using a language that was as elegant as any I can remember. I saved her letters for her. When she came back, from Alaska and from the long nights, she delighted in them. She was proud of the friendship she made with her depression, as well she should have been. I treasured the gift of both her elegant prose and her sharing the load with me. I asked her for the letters back, but she never sent them!

When it comes to the human record and to

friendship, simple, folksy letters are best. Small talk has great advantages. It greases the wheels of otherwise chaotic days, and reminds us of the depth in trivial events, providing a link between sacred and profane.

When it comes to what most people call profundity, letters also have virtue. They give us time to comprehend the weight of life. The March she had her breast removed, a friend of mine sent out a form letter, like the ones many people send at Christmas to update family and friends on their activities of the previous year. I would never have known the letter wasn't personally addressed to me; I did not mind the impersonality. I was delighted to be close even though far away. I used postcards to keep in touch with her on a regular basis—I knew I wasn't going to make time or have time for much more. But each postcard let me say something about her passage from one place to another. Those simple sentences will help me when I face sickness: I learned what I wanted to say under that duress.

Another friend, an actor, writes funny letters. They are tragicomic because I can always tell something bad has happened when one arrives. The first paragraph will be about losing the big part and getting the smaller one, or the latest idiocy of his director, or colleagues, or the American theater. Then he will salve his wound himself, by mining the event for the humor. If he can't find the humor, he will tell another funny story. Once I got a play-by-play description of a New York Mets game. So what if he was desperate? The letter made me laugh.

Mostly older people write letters. They don't like the telephone the way younger people do. I get letters from a half-dozen octogenarians, and I cherish each one. They come regularly; they get answered regularly. They keep me posted on what it means to get old.

I often cheat my own principle of slow and simple in letter writing. I will write one on the computer and personalize it to whoever has written me this week. (When you get a dozen letters a week, you have to do something to keep things moving along.) I always like to tell a couple of stories about the children. I like to talk about Warren, my husband, in an up-to-the-moment way. It helps me know him. I like to reflect on something big or important through the lens of some little thing that happened, like the day I wandered into the stained-glass repair shop, and cried because so much color has gone out of the church. Or the day the car broke down and no one but hoodlums offered to help. Or the day of the Oklahoma City bombing and how I had six children, my three and the neighbors' three, in the house, and how I ran to gather them up, feeling nearly ridiculous in my protection of children who, at that moment, were perfectly safe.

I have no doubt that if something horrible, like a death, illness, or break-in, happened, I would write letters about it. It would allow me to wade through the weight of life—and would all but guarantee that someone would talk back to me about it. Eventually.

Why write letters? To stay connected to people and to stay connected to depth. Given the ease with which letters accomplish that objective, it is hard to think of stamps as expensive. I imagine someday reading my old letters from my bench in the nursing home. They give me something to keep. Friendship takes keeping, as do we ourselves.

Letters also have a political purpose. I think of Antonio Gramsci, as I mentioned in the Introduc-tion, in his *Letters from Prison*. Gramsci is the one communist who may have been able to stop the wave of rigidity that swept over communism in the twentieth century. He failed, but his effort was absolutely brilliant—and we know of the effort from the letters. A Fascist prosecutor said at his trial, "We must prevent this brain from functioning for twenty years." Ironically, Mussolini's government accomplished just the opposite by imprisoning him and facilitating the prison notebooks. Gramsci—his teeth falling out, his stomach disintegrating, his arteries hardening prematurely, his headaches making him climb the walls, his insomnia giving him no more than three hours of fitful sleep a night for eleven years—still raced against time and wrote the reasons for opposition to what communism was becoming. He often had to write inadequate letters—to succumb to abstraction and ellipsis in the monumental notebooks. Still, the letters certify the ideas as both concretely lived and concretely lived by him, under the worst of circumstances. There is even some evidence that he may have forgiven the colleague who betrayed him and sent him to jail in the first place.

Gramsci wrote the things I want to know about. Who has struggled and why and how? Who got out of prison? Who stayed in? How did they manage while they were incarcerated? The answers to ques-

tions such as these inspire me.

It was a stint in jail, in fact, that turned me into a writer. Had I not been put in—I was there, in California, because I was protesting how lettuce was being grown—I never would have taken the time to write. Because of my good fortune, and especially because the Catholic activist Dorothy Day was a part of the group that was incarcerated at the time, I learned how delightful a stay "in" can be. There are freedoms in jail that don't exist elsewhere. We can think. We can imagine. We can write down our thoughts.

I'll never forget Dorothy's comment the day we were arrested. "Thank God," she said. "Now I can get caught up on my writing and my correspondence." A jail without paper and pencil would really be a jail. A jail with a pencil and paper is quite different. It is a place where letters can thrive.

I don't intend to demean the letter as a powerful political weapon. Well-written letters to a congressional representative or the kinds of letters that Amnesty International gathers to protest human rights violations and tortures have a powerful political purpose. I have personal labels made annually for each of my elected representatives and communicate with them as often as I can.

Rather, I mean that letters have also a deeper political purpose. They reveal to us or remind us of our own politics, which is much more important than letting someone else know them.

Letter writing is a peek below the surface of our life, down where our politics and our spirits and our friendships are forming. That level is like the soil, where things are really growing. Where seeds in another season, even now being prepared for underground, will break open and come forth. Where trouble now brewing will also break out. When we peek below the surface of our life, we get the lesson of development. Hearts open slowly. We need to pay attention to the stages of our life's development. Where are we now?

Writing a letter only has to answer that one

question to be successful. Put a date at the top of the paper and write.

Letters give us the chance to manage more of our friendships and more of politics and more of capacity than we otherwise really can. They open us to the stages of life, to its depth and the way it will change over time and take on new depth.

When we have friends and really share our truth with them, it changes the way things are from the inside out. Our letters describe the way we are changing. Letters capture the transient and the eternal, and that is why we write them.

When I advocate the writing of letters by middle-class Americans as a symbolic way to save our souls, I am referring to writing a letter from prison. The prison is the political and cultural economy of the first world. The great American comic writer James Thurber wrote about a character named Walter Mitty who escaped life in the suburbs, and about birds trapped in a cage, trapped in Sing Sing. We may not be able to fully escape every suburb or every Sing Sing, but we can get out from time to time. We can fly.

Because C. S. Lewis wrote letters, we know how much he loved his brother, what he really thought of God, and how death snuck up on him. His letters allow us to see how he evaluated his experience, and they encourage us to evaluate our own. Reflection on our experience is a time-honored way of escaping from it.

Because Vita Sackville-West and Harold Nicholson, the flashy Bloomsbury-group writers, corresponded constantly, writing more than ten thousand letters to each other in their long and often distant fifty-year marriage, we know a lot about a marriage that was anything but normal at the same time that it forged its own normality. We are inspired to make our own marriages more than they already are. Not only do we unlock doors to the unorthodox, but also we find ourselves walking through them into new and interesting rooms.

Because Reid Sherline collected dozens of let-ters written by many celebrated authors—including Samuel Johnson, Mark Twain, James Joyce, Marcel Proust, E. B. White, Edna St. Vincent Millay—to their mothers, we know a lot about parent-child relationships.

When Elizabeth Bishop writes to Marianne Moore, on September 11, 1940, "I scarcely know why I persist at all," we all gather in the front row of her private theater. We know her letter will explore her persistence and that she will answer herself—but probably only because she risked sharing her fatigue with Moore, her correspondent and trusted friend.

When Julia Ward Howe writes her friend that she is "tired, tired, tired, deep down into the next century," we are oddly comforted. We are not the only ones ever to be tired.

Letters disclose us to ourselves and to each other. It is at our great peril that we choose against such disclosure by letting the telephone or the Internet tell our stories. These fast, unrecorded methods tell our stories as though they were disposable. They are not. They need to be remembered, reread, resifted, rethought. Some of what we write is a costume, a wardrobe for the day and its mood. Other times, we get as close to the truth as we can. Without being able to access our own truth, and remember it, we are too easily colonized by the unelected royalties, the ones that make us move too fast to understand what is going on.

What are the consequences of not pondering our way through our oddly ordinary lives? Plane crashes are the consequences—personal, political, and spiritual plane crashes. Recently a spokesperson for the Federal Aviation Administration said that the actual cause of any plane crash is never single. "Always four or five things have gone wrong at the same time," he said, "and it is the interaction of the negativities that causes the plane to crash." Yes, indeed. In my life, too. Not just one thing. But the interaction of the negativities.

Letter writing pulls the tangled threads apart. It makes sense of them so they have less time to interact and cause trouble. Pondering in this way is primary prevention of trouble en route. The consequence of not pondering is to invite trouble.

Letter writing offers a period of tranquillity from which repose we heal ourselves and find our way to God. God? Where did God come from? From the tranquillity. Also in the political, the economic, the friendship, the trouble. God is in there. Hidden deeply, and waiting to be discovered.

Writing letters can give us the peace we seek; it can be the gateway to the profundity we covet.

From the inside out, our lives are full and gracious. Without pondering our experience, looking at it as though it were a fine gem, deserving of great attention, it is likely we will miss tranquillity and never make the acquaintance of repose.

Why write letters? To make the space for pondering. To keep our planes from crashing. To see deeply enough to see the largeness of our experience. To find God.

Write Letters Why
Why Wait? 10 Wa
ays to Simplify —
10 Ways and
Enjoy & Your

Chapter 2
why grow lettuce

EVERY TIME I EAT A BOWL OF ICEBERG LETTUCE, I VOW NOT TO EAT ANOTHER ONE. I CAN'T MANAGE TO KEEP THIS PROMISE BECAUSE I AM NOT YET PREPARED TO LEAVE SOCIETY. BUT I CAN AND DO FIND WAYS TO KEEP ICEBERG—AND ITS AGRICULTURAL ROOTS—OUT OF MY HOME. "AS LONG AS YOU'RE UNDER MY ROOF," MY MOTHER USED TO SAY, "YOU'LL DO WHAT I WANT YOU TO DO." SO SAY I TO LETTUCE.

Lettuce is just about the easiest thing in the world to grow. All it needs is soil that has been lightened by a pretty good combing. You can dig a plot six feet by six feet with your own hands in a week or two. Do it the

15

way kids do hard homework: Ten problems at a time. If you spend March combing and digging and preparing the soil, April sowing seed and thinning, you can spend May and June eating lettuce. The only heavy labor you'll need is turning over the soil. If you can't handle that yourself, hire someone. The price of a month's supply of iceberg balls is all it should cost you.

(If this whole project takes more than ten minutes a day, you are enjoying it too much. You will have become like one of those home bread bakers who use the dough as a hand massage. But the bread is a bonus pleasure to the wonderful salads you are about to eat.)

If your soil is not light enough after forking and combing—I prefer a three-pronged heavy hand tool for the combing—add a little peat or vermiculite. One bag should do.

Seed is available everywhere; black-seeded simpson is notorious for excellent germination. It is a bit weak as a leaf, and likes to collapse under the heavier salad dressings. Still, its color alone will make your first efforts worthwhile.

I like to plant a dozen varieties, ones I first picked up in Bergamo, Italy, where I developed an enduring envy of the way Italians eat. Now I can reorder these—and more—varieties through several domestic sources. Last year we had several arugulas,

French dandelion, red giant, red Russia kale, winter chervil, oak leaf, upland cress, mace, green mignonette, mizuna or mustard spinach (very spicy), and selma wisa.

I also planted one box calling itself mesclun after that variety at the grocery store known formerly to me as $9.98 a pound. Good as it was, I didn't see its virtue over the thinning I had been taking of my other varieties. And speaking of thinning, it is essential. As it grows, lettuce, particularly the heading varieties, doesn't like touching its neighbors. You may steal leaves from the balls as they grow to accomplish this process if nothing else manages the separation you need.

The salads we had for a full two months—because summer was kind and held off the heat until nearly August last year—were very spicy sometimes, very cool others. We could pick our favorites as long as we acknowledged which was about to bolt in the process. Bolting is the moment that lettuce says "Enough" and goes to seed. After that the plant just doesn't taste that good; although to stretch the season, it is no sin to include some old tough pieces in the bowl. Even they will rival iceberg—and you'll find yourself taking the same vow I have.

Why is iceberg such a crime? Because it arrives on our plate announcing that food is now being grown for the convenience of the market as opposed to the nourishment, body and soul, of the consumer. Like some of the tomatoes with which it often associates, iceberg is not really a food. It is a product. It has been grown for ease of shipping. It has used fossil fuels to get itself to you. It has almost no taste and even less nutrition. (The darker the leaf, the more vitamins it has.)

But don't think for a minute that someone else has done this to you. You have done this to yourself, by failing to grow what you could grow in your backyard, local park, or community garden. You want lettuce in the winter? Get grow lights or build a greenhouse. Or live like a person connected to the seasons and enjoy lettuce in the seasons that fit it, which

include both fall and spring. Leave it alone the rest of the time. There are winter vegetables. We pay much more for winter lettuce and winter tomatoes and winter oranges than we think we do. We pay for homogenization, so every season is like every other season, every town like every other town, every shopping mall like every other one, every meal the same, year in and year out. Variety is the opposite of homogenization here—and it costs much less than the iceberg in the first place.

The better lettuces will cost you, too, of course. As I've said, you have the possible one-time cost of labor if you're not strong enough to thatch or dig, and of course any soil additives you can't build yourself out of composting. (Composting is the art of piling your own food scraps on top of grass clippings, leaves, and other organic matters so that they become soil. It's great work, especially if you have ever feared death and decay. Here death and decay bear fruit.) The seed varieties are expensive, sometimes as high as two dollars a pack—which, by the way, is a little less than what they pay in France and Italy for similar seed. Add up what you pay for iceberg and then start subtracting. In money terms you'll come out about even.

But then use what Hazel Henderson, the great Canadian economist, calls "whole-cost accounting." What else did the iceberg cost you—in pleasure, nutrition, transport? In self-respect?

There is a cost in embarrassment also. When we don't get involved in our own food production and purchasing at the "front end," the production end, we become just consumers. We don't want to be just consumers. We don't want, as one man said to me, to be "just a checkbook." We don't want to fail our best selves. We don't want to be used by big markets. Whenever I eat an iceberg salad, I feel ashamed. I failed again to eat the way I want to eat. I want to have control over my taste buds, my nutrition, my pleasure, my economy. I rue my salad days and their passing yet again. And then I compost my distaste. I plow it back in and go out and give my lettuce patch an extra caress. Even if there is snow on the ground, there is nothing wrong with giving a feed of manure or compost. The snow carries it down nicely.

These rituals help my vow along. Religiously, you might say. Is such a religious attitude appropriate with respect to lettuce? You bet it is. Lettuce is certainly not God but God created a world of such great variety and beauty that we dare not reduce it. Iceberg is reductionist in the worst sense of the word. Growing our own lettuce is the opposite. As such, it is liturgy. It is service. It is co-creative. It is praise, offertory, proclamation, and confession wrapped in one, like a good Sunday morning worship. It is respect for the original garden. It is parabolic—not

that it changes the world, but it shows us how we could if we would.

And oh, those salads! Those salad days.

It would not be impossible to use this strategy of "growing your own" at the community level. Many people have tried through the community-supported agricultural movement. They have had outstanding local success, which is all the success they wanted in the first place. There is no need to turn local economic self-help into a conglomerate.

Here in Amherst, we are part of the Western Massachusetts Food Bank through its farm in Hadley, down the road. That food bank feeds thousands of people throughout the area. We pay four hundred dollars per year for a family share in the farm. That puts the farmer into business in the spring. He grows food for us and our family and food for the food bank for nearly nine months of the year. We get the pleasure of knowing that what some call our "yuppified" tastes (and we call our good taste) are being satisfied by some of the finest organic vegetables in the world. The Connecticut River runs right by the farm; the area is widely understood as having some of the best soil in the world. We also get the pleasure of knowing that the poor are also getting the best. And we see the corn come in, slowly, kernel by kernel, when we pick up our bags every Friday.

In contrast to this delightful experience, I remember the supermarkets on the west side of Philadelphia and the south side of Chicago. I remember the vegetables well. I could swear that somebody took them out of the truck and stomped on them before putting them on the shelves. The difference between city vegetables and rural vegetables was astonishing. If I drove out of the city, even a little way, I could find much fresher vegetables at much lower cost.

The joy of the poor in soup kitchens, who much too often get leftovers, getting the first and best fruits is something I find deeply moving. That's why we belong to the food bank farm. The joy of feeding the poor as well as you feed yourself—and feeding yourself as well as the poor are fed—is such that I simply can't understand why so many people say community-supported agricultural projects are too "expensive."

Why grow lettuce at a communal level? To feed the poor and to feed them well. To give poor people jobs so they can feed themselves. The methods of mechanization and computerization and standardization—which are the methods of the food industry—will keep our food costs low and our possibility of food jobs even lower. It will also further destroy our food. Even more pesticides will be needed to protect these methods against surprises.

I am reminded of the idea of destroying the village in order to save it. I am astonished that most Americans want cheap food instead of good food. According to the Campaign for Sustainable Agriculture, the average dinner travels fourteen hundred miles from farm to table. That is a long way to go for cheap, stale food.

One of the first jobs I ever had was as an outreach worker for the Office of Economic Opportunity. I was supposed to find and tabulate the poor in Adams County, Pennsylvania. Every day I went out in my government-supported car and found people and counted them. I also talked to them.

One couple, the Kemps, about seventy and both skinny as rails, lived in a one-room shack on the edge of a farmer's field. He "never moved us off," the man said, "so we stayed." They had a freezer, a bed, a stove, and a lot of piles of old papers that served as insulation as well as decoration.

When I came to the part in my questionnaire about how they ate, they told me, "Well." I assumed they would tell me about hunting stories, which they did. (One twenty-three-year-old mother of three who lived in a similar circumstance told me about waiting all day long for about a month every year to "kill me a deer." She just sat still and waited for one to come. She didn't have the courage to track them.) The Kemps told me about rabbits they had caught and eaten. But then Mrs. Kemp told me the real secret to their longevity: dandelions. Every spring they gathered and froze dandelion greens, right before they bloom their ubiquitous yellow. They ate them all winter, and that made them "the healthiest poor folk around," as she said.

I have eaten from the dumpsters at the big grocery stores. I have learned what days they put the yogurts in, what days the bread goes out, what days to wait at dawn for the miscellaneous excess of a mostly overweight society. I could have eaten from my own checkbook but I found the intrigue of garbage, and its waste, too compelling.

Why grow lettuce? Because eating products from agribusiness is not really eating. It is disconnection from our food. It is alienation from our land.

Walter Brueggemann, the Hebrew Scripture scholar, writes that owning our own land is precisely what the Hebrew Scriptures are all about. Whenever food comes to us from far away, from someone else's land, you can bet, in this political economy, that some injustice has been involved. I learned that in the lettuce fields of California a long time ago when, along with many others, I was jailed for protesting what migrant workers had to suffer while tending lettuce.

Injustice is not essential to growing food: we could pay more for our food and make its production and distribution more just. But we do not make those choices. We prefer the low price at the store. Fast, more, and most have become our values; we eat those values. And our food tastes like them.

In Europe, the Common Market is threatening to pasteurize cheese. It has already done so in most places. By regulating the cream content in the famous French, smelly cheeses, the Common Market has destroyed levels and layers of taste and variety. Much is already gone. Fortunately, an underground market survives, and some excellent cheese is still made and sold. When I asked a knowledgeable restaurateur in France whether younger people were going into this underground market, he told me no. "There is no money in it," he said. "People won't pay that much for cheese."

Paying more for our food is one option that both

makes for justice and makes for excellence. Another option is to go even more local and to become more knowledgeable about food and growing and cooking. We could learn to farm at local levels and cut out the packaging, the middle people, the trucking, and the managing. (Our family raised goats for some time to get French cheese. We never learned how to get even close to the good stuff, but our yogurt was fantastic.) Growing and making our own is a way we could get less expensive, still good food. We could feed our own communities. No, we could not have the variety we now have. But we could have much of it. We could have chokecherry jelly instead of the ubiquitous strawberry in packages that travel well and are square and stack neatly, depressing me, which is another cost in this whole business.

How do we get better jelly? How do we get jelly back in a jar, with a spoon, even? Go to the edges of the field and find a few berries and jell them. In general, smaller fields and corners of fields could be mined for their bounty; it wouldn't be so necessary to grow or move in bulk.

Now that so many of us eat most of our meals from fast food, in containers that travel, we are even farther away from soil, from dandelions, from growth. Americans are notorious throughout the world for eating bad food. With our over-refrigerated, under-smelled food, hygienic to a fault, we don't eat as well as many people in the third and fourth worlds. They at least still know how to cook for themselves.

There is a poignant sculpture by Raymond Mason in the cathedral St. Eustace in Les Halles in Paris. Les Halles is where the outdoor market used to be; in 1969 it was moved to the suburbs. Now a large franchised mall takes it place. Inside the cathedral is a sculpture of food stalls and French workers, with an inscription that remembers "the depart of the fruits and vegetables from the heart of Paris." It is hard to imagine fully the sculpture's grief because most people in Paris still shop daily, using baskets, at outdoor neighborhood markets. Compared to our "progres-sive" supermarkets, the French still have it made. They can touch and see and carry their food. They are still pre-packaging, pre-cellophane.

Why grow lettuce? As resistance to the "super market." As a way to keep fruits and vegetables in the heart of our cities. As a way to play with our work, to enjoy the production of our own food. As a way to give our checkbook a rest. As a way to get to know our own taste buds. For the poor. For the community. For cheese. For the dirt under our fingernails and the smells that linger.

Why grow lettuce? Because homegrown lettuce is good to eat.

Chapter 3
why sing songs

I DON'T REMEMBER HOW MY FAMILY MANAGED TO PAY FOR PIANO LESSONS FOR ME, BUT THEY DID. THEY COULD HAVE SAID THEY COULDN'T AFFORD IT. MY LOCAL SCHOOL IS NOW TELLING ME THEY CAN'T AFFORD MUSIC—WHICH, AT LEAST AS THEY SEE IT, IS TRUE. INSTEAD OF MUSIC BEING SOMETHING THAT ALL CHILDREN MAY TAKE IN GRAMMAR SCHOOL, IT WILL BE DONE BY FEE FOR SERVICE— FIFTY DOLLARS PER CHILD PLUS THE INSTRUMENT RENTAL. THUS SAITH THE SCHOOL BOARD.

When I was liberated from daily piano practice, I rejoiced. Free time always has appeal to the child and the child within us. But when I hear other people playing the piano, I go green. They seem so happy. I'd gladly trade all my free time for the ability to play one piece of Bach. I'd trade a lot more than that if music and money weren't so gruesomely related. Do I have a chip on my shoulder about this and other injuries of class? Yes. It is so big that it actually interferes with my fingering.

Memories such as these will cause me to pay the fifty dollars, but before I write my check, I want to go on record. I'm going to sing anyway. Whether I pay per note or not.

Music has been invaded by class. Its purity is less today than it was yesterday in my children's schools. That the competition for funds is between a more organized environmental lobby and a less organized music lobby—as it is here—doesn't elevate the conversation one bit. Environmentalists know what happens when a price tag gets put on everything. They should fear their own victory: when environment poises against music and wins, something is deeply wrong.

Not that music has ever been that free or pure. Princes paid for it when kings didn't in the Renaissance period. Ask any church organist what she has to go through to get a decent prelude in. Or ask any music teacher how pure her parents are in their respect for her profession. But, allowing this typical amount of impurity, why would the school board want to add to it? I can almost hear the crumbling of the local commitment to music and to the kind of culture it represents. Right before my very ears.

Soon we will remember even more the way ears can delight at good sound. But it is precisely we who need to disconnect music from money! No one keeps us from keeping our vocal cords in shape.

I remember going into a worship service late at a conference. The woman in the back row was already singing, in an unbelievable monotone. She did the courteous thing and offered to share her hymnbook with me, pointing to the place we were in the hymn. We carried on together, me in my mono-tone and she in hers, and I realized that we were exemplars of grace. You can sing without singing well. Churches have always provided back rows just for that.

I did lean toward the other singers so that they could raise my voice—in the same way that I tilt away from people with bad breath—but I enjoyed knowing that there was at least one person in the world who sang worse than I did. She seemed to enjoy it nonetheless, the same way I do. Music has less to do with excellence than with elevation. Uplift. The spirit of it all.

We who spend time updating our equipment, from eight-track tapes to cassettes to compact discs, who spend over ten dollars for each experience we now can't play, have choices. We could sing our own songs. Take voice lessons every day, self-administered, in our cars and at our clotheslines. We could hum when we get really uptight. We could sing our hearts out in our own church choirs and there—for no fee—learn music. Or for our next party we could have a sing-along. Focus on folk songs, civil rights songs, old hymns, or blood hymns. The quality of our sound matters less than that we sing. There really is no such thing as a wrong note.

No one keeps our vocal cords from throbbing, no matter how high the price goes on music lessons. We can teach ourselves to sing and to ally ourselves with others who know how to sing.

I remember walking into a French cathedral in the country. I was in a jaded mood that said there is no point in "another church." How could I have known that people were practicing for the European Bach Festival of Organs in that place at that very time? Eight o'clock in the morning on a weekday. When I opened the heavy church door, I heard a sound that can never be duplicated. It had a fullness and a sweetness that even my uneducated ear understood. Power. God. Grace.

Now, when I watch the active decline of music in schools and society, when I watch the organist shortage increase in our churches, I comfort myself with this knowledge. Even when music is turned off for me, and my kind of people, it is still playing somewhere. Behind an old cathedral door. In a remote village. Humanity won't let music go. Some will still play and practice. When I suggest a populist strategy for music, that we sing our own songs, I am suggesting a stewardship of music. I am suggesting that we join these European organists in saving music—even if the only melody we are saving is one we recall from the Beatles.

We were staying overnight at the home of a close, upper-class friend. The night had been long and good. Three o'clock in the morning had appeared out of nowhere. As we climbed into our bed upstairs in the old Vermont farmhouse, a lullaby glided off the piano keys. A personal serenade. A moment when music made its peculiar meaning and etched its drama into our wooden parts or the parts of us that are frozen shut. Meltdown. Then sleep.

Also present was my jealousy. My class hostility. Because of the loveliness of the evening, though, I was able to overcome the covetousness and move with the music. I wonder how many people will even be able to play lullabies once the pricers get done with the school system. I wonder what will happen to surprise, goosebumps, meltdowns. Will we be all wooden parts? Will all our parts freeze up?

This horror story happens if we don't sing and

play ourselves. It is prevented by the simple act of making our own music—returning to that place where music came from. No, Virginia, it did not come from the record store. Music came from people.

People have always made music, with or without schools. Duke Ellington learned how to play off the band without a teacher. Bessie Smith managed to sing the blues. Old women in hot apartment buildings, summer nights, hum. Children jump rope to songs that are as deep as rivers. Churches and synagogues fill up with hymns.

We don't have to have schools to instruct children in music. Churches could do it. But churches should see that if they keep paying their organists 1950s salaries, people will not continue to invest the dozen years or so it takes to learn the organ. We will see that our own cheapness is the cause of musical poverty.

Not that all people allow price tags to cow them so. Many people have found their way to music all by themselves. But what is it that they are teaching in schools that could be so much more important than the organ or the piano or well-exercised vocal cords?

The children hurt by this new and cheap decision will be neither the poor nor the rich. They will be the middle children, of what we used to call the middle class. The not-so-poor-enough to get aid.

The richer children will still find their way to music. Their parents will know its value.

Part of the populist lifestyle is to know that we are rich, even though we're not. It is to do what many poor mothers already do—they dress their children as though they were rich so that the children won't experience prejudice. Those of us who are musically poor and don't have a song in our heart may pretend that we are rich enough to afford good music. And in that pretense, we will become rich. You're only as poor, musically, as you think you are.

The generations of people who grew up with popular music can tell us about music that is for sale and is also something more. Music is beyond sale. I think of Aristedes, who wrote in the spring 1995 issue of *American Scholar*:

> *In America of the 1940s and 1950s, when I was growing up, popular music was everywhere; and it was not of interest only to the young, as popular music is today. Singers were great heroes; bandleaders famous personages. At a neighborhood delicatessen in Rogers Park called Ashkenaz, there was a sandwich called the Lou Breese, named after the bandleader at the Chicago Theater. I don't recall the contents of that sandwich but I feel confident it must, by today's standards, have*

been powerfully life threatening: chopped liver
and pastrami, perhaps. I do know, though,
that I would rather have a sandwich named
after me than receive an honorary degree from
any university in the Western world.[1]

Nowadays music is more like a gourmet restaurant than a sandwich. It is more available to those who can pay for it and buy it and put it on their personal compact discs than to those who cannot.

Aristedes remembers what he calls "the sheer musicality of life." He recalls the serenading of fraternities, grade-school pageants, and novelty songs like "Mairzy Doats"; "I can still do a full rendition of the 'Purple People Eater' today," he brags. (So can I.) He reports that Gershwin on his deathbed whispered just one word: "Astaire." Then he confesses that "Intellectuals don't dance," and pokes fun at the contrast between the intellectual life and the life of musical romance. "In musical romance," he claims, "only the unexamined life is worth living."

Aristedes also makes a new distinction for history: B.R. or A.R.—Before Rock or After Rock. This, he contends, is "one of the great, perhaps uncrossable, divisions of humankind. Those of us who came before cannot hope and, let us speak candidly, do not all that much wish to understand the musical tastes of those who came after." I wish I could speak personally with him and tell him how important rock and roll is to me, how it has gotten me through the worst moments of my life, how "Dancin' in the Streets" came on once when I was in Budapest and I saw God.

Some intellectuals do dance. Not enough of them. But some. One friend of mine, who would not call himself an intellectual but probably is, organizes dancing at all our national church meetings, which don't get many people to dance. (That is not completely true: we did publish a new hymnal in the United Church of Christ that many refer to as close to the only joy mainline Protestants can find today.)

Some people are like Gershwin, who died at age thirty-nine, and "lived all his life in youth," as S. N. Behrman puts it in *People in a Diary*. My friend, who organizes the dancing at otherwise sterile hotel complexes, is living in a youth he has misplaced but not lost. My own parents still go out dancing on Saturday night. At age sixty-seven my mother broke her arm missing a twirl on the dance floor. She is back at it, and has been for years.

As much as I love rock and roll, and as much as I love my section in this wild century, I am still jealous of my parents' generation for its music. "But if the Gershwins and others wrote songs that had about them the spirit of youth," Aristedes continues, "it was youth of a different kind than we have come to associate with being young. It was youth untroubled, full of promise, agonizing over nothing greater than winning that boy or girl . . . even chimpanzees do it (argues youth)." He confirms my reasons for being jealous.

What is Aristedes doing with his spare time today? Not dancing, apparently, although if he would ever like to go out, I am available. He is memorizing "Stars Fell on Alabama" and the entire Gershwin corpus. He uses the lyrics as mantras. So goes one man down the street singing, "See the pyramids along the Nile . . ." I can imagine another joining him with "The world will always welcome lovers." My imagination continues intergenerationally: "I can't get no satisfaction . . . ," followed by "Lay, lady, lay . . ." For a finale we could all do "Purple People Eater" together. The streets could be even more beautiful than they already are.

I haven't even given hymns their full due here. Hymns, for some of us, bridge the periods before and after rock and roll. Absolutely nothing has the power that a hymn has to unfreeze the ice in our veins. On Easter, when the faithful raise the strain of triumphant gladness, or on silent, holy nights—at these times, the devil and its demons have nothing to say or do. There is no room in our souls for them even to maneuver.

When my son Jacob was born, he was premature, as was his twin sister, Katie. She had enough lung, he did not. He spent the first week of his life hooked up to a respirator. On the day that he was to be let off the respirator, we were prepared for really good things, but also for really bad things. I sang Easter hymns as I held his little body and all those tubes in my arms and the doctor turned off the machine, letting him breathe real air. We were in the neonatal intensive care unit of Northwestern Hospital in Chicago. Dozens of other equally ill babies were very close by. As we left that day, many other mothers and fathers thanked me for singing. It helped them to hear me.

The best night of my life was at a New York ball-room where the Gay Men's Chorus was having a party. Someone gave me some extra tickets at the last minute. There I was, being a wallflower, dressed in anything but my ball gown, while everyone else was dressed in theirs—and I do mean almost every-one. A man in his early seventies and a suit approached me in my thirties and blue jeans. "Would you like to dance?"

I would love to dance. And to sing. No one needs to name a sandwich after me. But when I go to sleep, I hope there will be a lullaby. Either that, or dancing in the streets. It doesn't even have to be a brand-new beat.

Why sing songs? Because you can't dance forever.

Write Letters Why
Why Wait Wa
ays to Simplify —
10 Ways and
Enjoy + Your Li

Chapter 4
why keep house

WHEN MY GRANDMOTHER DIED IT WAS MY JOB TO CLEAN OUT HER HOUSE. IN HER ATTIC I FOUND THOUSANDS OF RUBBER BANDS TIED TOGETHER AND LABELED. EVERY BULLETIN FROM THE IMMANUEL LUTHERAN CHURCH THAT WAS WRITTEN IN HER LIFETIME WAS TIED IN A NEAT PACKAGE WITH STRING AROUND IT. THERE WERE ALSO DOZENS OF STRING BALLS, MADE FROM THE EXCESS STRING.

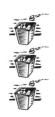

Likewise there were homemade notepads, consisting of stacks of scrap paper cut out of junk mail. And pencil stubs. Christmas wrap for the ages. She had not wasted a thing. Some Tuesdays when I take my two garbage cans and my recycling box out to

39

the curb, I think of her and what she would think of me.

I remember Don Hall's poem "String Too Short to Be Saved," from that box that he found in his grandfather's attic. He saw the poetic humor in his find just as I see the irony in my garbage compared to my grandmother's garbagelessness. I thank God that individually we are part string too short to be saved. But we are connected; salvation is what all flesh must see together. On this highfalutin principle I forgive myself my garbage cans and their waste. And wait with all flesh, to see, together. I join Hall's grandfather, my grandmother, and Hall himself, and "keep house" my way.

My way involves a housekeeper who comes in every two weeks and cleans the house. He works alone, he is fast, he is careful, and I can tell when he has come because the desks all have little pieces of change and old scraps of paper on them. I never know how I can live so carelessly that money and paper disappear and I don't even know they are gone—and my grandmother could have lived, and died, without losing a thing. I keep reminding myself that we are cut from the same cloth but wear entirely different dresses. She was an old-fashioned woman whose year was marked by spring cleaning and fall cleaning. I am a new-fashioned one and never pick up a vacuum. I pay some of what I earn outside the house to have the house cleaned. (For a long period I shared the housework, rather tediously, with my husband. I even told my sons that "girls" weren't supposed to vacuum, and it is a bit of a household joke that I *tidy* but my housecleaner really *cleans*.)

While I give the most minimal of my resources to housecleaning, there is nothing I love more than a clean house. Fresh flowers on the coffee table are something I cherish—and when they overstay and become brown or limp, I find myself deeply embarrassed. What if my grandmother saw them?

Sometimes I even ball my string. It is a way of honoring my grandmother. She could use a lot more honor from me. I have demoted what she thought was a woman's priority. I have moved it down the list to at least second or third place.

At least weekly I make fun of churches that can only think about their buildings and their upkeep. Then I go home and hassle my house into order. I nick the edges the way Goose Gossage used to pitch to the plate. Fast. Furious. Aiming for the outside. What do people mean when they say "my house is a mess"? Is this an edifice complex? Something stupid and silly? Or is there something noble about our love for our space? Our shell? Our bodies? Should I repent my disdain for churches that are edifice oriented?

If I believe in the incarnation at all, I should. If I believe in aesthetics, I should. If I believe in beauty, I should. It is hard to get incarnation or aesthetics or beauty without paying attention to our bodies. Some now call it embodiment: if our house is a mess, are we not embodying mess? If our houses are well kept, are we not embodying the value of well-keptness?

With three children in the house, plus friends, plus equipment, keeping house is nearly impossible for me. But I surely don't want to relinquish housekeeping forever. It's too important to me.

Through my church/home hypocrisy, I have become acquainted with a demon. Its name is a blessed rage for order in a world that can't be controlled. Another is control—despite my acquaintance with its shadow side. A third is facing a room that has just been picked up but now has a human being rearranging it to his or her liking, which often means beverages, magazines, cards, cats, opened mail, and a sweatshirt that used to be needed.

Knowing at least some of my own complexity, I wonder why the great biblical quarrels in the country today surprise me or anyone. The fundamentalist movement is wonderful precisely because of its tendency to be awful. Like my house, or control, or order, it delights and frightens—and keeps us humble. We don't always say all that we mean. Sometimes we say more than we mean. With St. Paul, the good that we would do, we don't, and the evil that we would not do, we do. You should see my basement. Or at least take a good long look at your own. Criticism, even when temperately universal, is always dangerous—which is why we should always apply it most to ourselves. And after we've cleaned our own house, or made fun of our own theology, or caused our own grandmother to turn over in her grave, we can then dare comment on fundamentalists or our neighbor's house. Once we have thrown our son's sweatshirt in the garbage can, lest it appear on our just-swept floor one more time, we can be humble in our outrage at other people's rigidity.

When I criticize fundamentalists, I tend to believe that I am "more biblical than thou." It is the same halo with which I clean: I am cleaner than thou, more caring than thou, neater than thou. In cleaning and criticism, I resemble that new book with the title *The Dictatorship of Virtue*. My husband actually gave me a tape of Wagner's "The Ride of the Valkyries" to use as theme music. I am more certain of my spoke than I am of yours and more able to see your spoke than I am able to see mine. So sure I am that Jesus loves the poor, especially, that I mistrust anyone who doesn't say so in the first few minutes of any speech. Eurocentric interpretations, despite their glory in the martyrdom of Bonhoeffer or the strictness of Barth or the brilliance of Bultmann, frighten me. The cheese was always too good where they wrote. A few days of humbler fare—tortillas, perhaps—would have helped each of them, and would help me, to know more of Christ.

In the first chapter of Mark there is a great short story about Jesus. He heals many people at Simon's house, then goes on to "cast out many demons." Clearly he knew that they were legion, although we don't know how he developed this maturity. The important thing is that the way he cast out the demons was by knowing their names.

Health comes, I believe, by knowing the names of the things that get in its way. Anxiety. Taking self too seriously. Ponderousness in daily challenge to lightness. Order. Control. Instead of being biblical,

we make our goal being "more biblical than thou." Instead of just cleaning our house, we try to clean it in terms of some outer standards. *Better Homes and Gardens.* Or the woman next door. Or Grandma.

The other demon is nearly the opposite of these. It is the demon of thinking we can live well without fresh flowers on the table. If one demon takes too much care for tidiness, the other takes too little. Why clean house? To plot a path between the demons.

All this humility, by the way, either attaches to some boldness or becomes the demon whose name, when not "sloppy," is "wishy-washy." The ground for boldness is that great Reformation advice to sin boldly. Make mistakes. Our rectitude is not that important anyway. Nor is it required of us that we *always* plot a path between the demons. Sometimes our house is a mess and needs to be that way. Sometimes our house is too orderly and needs to be that way too. Sinning boldly means having less fear of the demons.

I love the advice of the Florida governor who has asked people to experiment with health insurance possibilities. He says he is giving a prize to the best innovation and also to the worst, precisely to encourage experimentation. In this social policy, he is battling the demon of perfectionism and encouraging the virtue of risk. I wish I could give a house-cleaning prize in a similar way. A prize for the most creative way to keep the modern clutter cleaned up—whatever "cleaned up" may mean.

My husband and I tried to raise our children without letting them have guns. They have turned everything from a loaf of French bread to their fingers into guns. If our children, innocent as they are, can turn bread into guns, then surely so-called Christians can turn the Bible into a battering tool. Good housewives can turn our own clean houses into judgments against others, particularly our children. If all we ever say to them is, "Pick up your socks," they think obedience is our goal. Instead, responsibility is our goal. We want our children to learn to keep things well, not just to do as they are told. When responsibility and obedience get confused in child raising, usually it is the demons messing about within us. As Elizabeth Crary points out in *Pick Up Your Socks: A Practical Guide to Raising Responsible Children*, responsibility and obedience are different. Both are necessary, but in different situations. We dare not be naive about what the demons can and will do to mess up our houses and our children's homes.

You can even imagine the delight of other parents who always found us a little "holier than thou" on the gun issue. They have capitulated to the demon within humility—which delights when the other falls. This self-righteousness is what some parts of us will feel when other parts of us stumble—when the children of Mrs. Squeaky Clean get themselves into big trouble.

What Mark is trying to tell us in describing Jesus' method of healing is that to be well we may accept our own demons. Don't think for a minute that we don't have them. To stay well we may get acquainted with the demons. Know them by their names.

Demons within demons within demons. Each offering us, oddly, health, even salvation, if we can get to know them, and by knowing them know ourselves, and our salvation. This happens in places as normal, ordinary, and messy as Simon's house. Demons abound. In getting to know their names, we can heal ourselves. Or at least protect ourselves from the horror of hypocrisy.

Most houses, most days, are a mess. Most days my life resembles a tangle. Commitment A is sitting on top of commitment B and I can't seem to get untied from commitment C. "Caught" is my middle name, "knotted" the description of experience I use most often. That's why I love *The Ashley Book of Knots*. It gives some of the finer knots a name, and actually teaches how to tie them—and untie them. Grandma's ball of string did the same things. It put the mess together. It was an attempt at order. Not a success, but an attempt. I clean house for the same reason she balled string: to attempt order.

Making friends with the tangle is not a bad spiritual strategy. That could be another reason to save string. To honor the knottedness. To honor the clutter. And to honor Grandma, all at the same time.

Write Letters Why

Why Wait 10 Ways to Simplify —

10 Ways and

Enjoy + Your Life

Chapter 5

A FRIEND WAS PICKING UP HER SON AT OUR HOUSE ONE AFTERNOON ABOUT FIVE O'CLOCK. IT WAS ONE OF THOSE OLYMPIC PICKUPS WE DRIVERS KNEW WELL THAT TERRIBLY SEVERE WINTER. SNOW BANKS. NO MARGIN TO THE ROAD. FIVE DEGREES BELOW ZERO. SHE HAD HER FOUR-YEAR-OLD AND HER SIX-YEAR-OLD IN THE CAR WITH HER. SHE MISSED OUR HOUSE AND GOT DISORIENTED.

Not knowing the neighborhood very well and loath to return, she pulled into a driveway down the street from us. She took the two children out of the car with her because the driveway was quite steep and her emergency brake unreliable. She knocked on the door of our neighbors' house only to discover two older people peeping through their windows at her. They never opened the door for her question about directions. They just stood at the window and stared. She reports that there was every reason to believe that they could not only see her but see the two children as well. It was dusk but not deeply dusk.

I am now referring to the time before this incident as B.F.: Before Fear. And the time since it as P.F.: Post Fear. I heard the story of the woman in Worcester who locked herself outside in the cold and then froze to death because no one would let her in. I suppose I expect that sort of thing in Worcester, sorry to say. But this far outside the big, bad city?

Here, in Amherst, we don't even lock our doors. Not that my family ever did, except in Chicago and Paris. And there the major inconvenience of the day was unbolting, unlocking, rebolting, relocking. (I'll never forget one apartment we had in Paris—four locks on the door. It took five minutes to get in and out, after you learned it.)

B.F. I traveled the entire region of western Massachusetts without fear. I simply assumed that if I broke down someone would take me in. Once I did break down, in Springfield, which is a fairly large city, and ended up knocking on the door of a pajama-clad man in his fifties. He didn't ask a single question as he pointed to his phone. He had just started a video; the popcorn was still warm, and he offered me some. I have always expected this kind of hospitality from everyone. I offer it; I expect it. It makes me feel safe.

Now I wonder. My own neighbors scared me. Now I see that I have become a bit like Kitty Genovese, perhaps the most famous victim of unneighborliness. Out there on my own.

Kitty Genovese was murdered in front of her neighbors in Queens on March 13, 1964. The neighbors, dozens of them—the only ones who could have saved her—did not. I imagine the same fate coming to my endangered neighbors. If I do not do my part to watch out for them, then nobody watches out for

them. If they are not watching over me, then nobody watches over me.

What happened to my neighbors to frighten them so? What turned them from neighbors and door openers into window peepers? One too many shovels lifted from their garage? Excessive reading of the police digest? Too much late-night news? Or something truly terrible, something they don't speak about to others? Something that locked first their hearts and then their doors? I know these things do happen. I also know that if our reaction closes doors, things can only get worse. Oddly, the more untrustworthy some of our neighbors become, the more trustworthy others, even strangers, must become.

I do lock the door sometimes when my husband is away. I get a certain ridiculous comfort from it. It seems to be another form of tucking the children in. But the idea of a lock making one safe strikes me as absurd. We have been broken into a few times in our married life—and each time the criminal got in another way than through the unlocked door.

This leads me to the reason we shouldn't fret with locks. Lock away, if it makes for comfort. But locking dare not be a source of safety. Safety, by the way, has the same root as the Hebrew word *shalom*, peace. Safety is also the root of salvation. Saved. Secure. These are religious experiences before they are physical experiences. They are matters of trust.

Of being connected to our own ground and our own ground of being. And of being connected to the land, the spot, the house we live in—belonging to it, not letting other people mess with it. Of being allowed to live where we are. Having deep permissions: what belongs to us belongs to us. No one invades that. What happens to our stereos or shovels matters less to us than the community and the land that surround us. These no one can steal. They are basic.

The crime issue has become a matter of great misinterpretation. We utter such clichés as "I can't even be safe in my own living room anymore." But we are not meant to be safe in our living rooms. It is an absurd goal, a ridiculous destination. The place of safety is the common place, the streets. The Hebrew Scriptures tell us to restore streets to dwell in (Isa. 58:12). When streets are safe, then living rooms will also be so. It's not that there is anything wrong with wanting a little peace in our own living rooms, but making that our objective belittles our safety. We are due more than that. Much more.

We are due shalom. Peace. Security and salvation. Safety is being saved. The great religions of the world know at least this about salvation, about safety, about peace. It is something all flesh see together. It is something held in common. Not suburb by suburb, neighborhood fortress by neighborhood fortress.

It is not only ethically wrong to elevate living room safety to a virtue; it is also the height of impracticality.

Every person in prison costs taxpayers at least thirty-eight thousand dollars per year. That would be enough to hire a neighborhood watch organizer for every community in the United States. Every study shows that neighborhood watches work. *Not* watching invites the criminals. Neighborhoods are safe when we know each other well enough to keep the crooks out. Ourselves. Without guns. You might call it the liberal's vigilante squad.

Streets for dwelling involve neighborhoods taking back the power to know each other, *and* it involves developing worlds where criminals can find work besides crime. Can be safe. Can *have* living rooms. Both prevention and prevention, not prevention and punishment, as the new slogan goes.

Individualism and its pal, centralization, enjoy big success by destroying communities. They don't mean to; they just do. They trick us into thinking that we must fight our enemies either as individuals—the micro-micro-strategy in which we are all alone with our personal weapon—or as nations, the macro-macro-strategy of the nuclear bomb. Each gives up on the one thing that could actually work, which is the right setting for problems to be solved. That setting is local, face-to-face community. We might call it neighborhood vigil-antes. Looking out for each other—before we have to be condemned to peeping as a way of life—is as good a strategy for self-protection as I can imagine.

Lots of us have been involved in "Take Back the Night" marches. We acknowledge there some of what I am saying here. We have given away the night—and there have been thugs standing by to take it. None of what I say here gives the thugs a break. They are more irresponsible than we—in the sense that they also ignore their own shalom, their own salvation. They act insecurely and take what doesn't belong to them, sometimes even innocent people's lives. But we behave insecurely when we peep out of our windows, lock ourselves up, imagine security in just our own living rooms. We behave irresponsibly toward the larger matters of securing our own safety. Our safety comes from living as though we belonged on our land and in our neighborhood, not remote as strangers.

Most of the time, I think of my neighborhood with great appreciation. Next door is an Iranian-American, part-Muslim, part-Jewish, family of four adults and a half-dozen children. It is a great privilege for my Jewish/Christian family to have another interfaith grouping next door. It keeps things interesting.

One Saturday the children were all in our house, playing those kinds of jumping-up-and-down games that children love to play on the furniture. We had to go out for about an hour, and so we put an eleven-year-old in charge. It was the first time he had been given such great responsibility. It became his job to stop the jumping and start some other activity. We trusted their children and we trusted ours, and we were only going to be gone a short while. The furniture and the children would be safe.

Our appointment ran late, so I called home and got Cyrus, the six-year-old from next door, on the phone.

"Hello, let me speak to Isaac." Isaac is our calm, cool, collected babysitter.

"You can't."

"Why not?"

"Because he's not here."

"Where is he?"

"At his house. This is my house."

"No, Cyrus, that is my house.
　　You are at my house."

"Oh, no, this is my house."

"No, it is not."

"Whoops, I forgot."

I love the fact that he forgot whose house he was at. We should all be so lucky as children, that we have many houses where we think we belong. I did

as a child. But very few children have that luxury today, unless parents are paying an hourly fee for the hospitality.

There is real danger in some neighborhoods. Some we cause by a smaller carelessness, like not paying attention or not sending food when someone is sick, and others we cause by a larger carelessness, like not voting or not being informed on public issues. What is the solution? To care more. To care more actively and more locally.

I have been able, sort of, to make friends with the people who first caused me to become afraid on the street where I live. I dropped by their yard sale— and now we at least speak, even though we don't say much. They did not come to our last backyard potluck, organized on the spur of the moment. The other older couple down the street came; so did the next-door crowd and the people across the street.

They, by the way, keep both their own son and another child every other weekend. The other boy lives with his mother during the week, his father on weekends. Every other weekend, the father comes up from Washington and stays at the Howard Johnson's with the child. The father and son also stay across the street the intervening weekend. They are a part of our neighborhood, even though they don't live here. His son sees the June bugs with ours. He is part of the soccer game on the grass when the adults gath-

er. He enjoys our outdoor fireplace with the "neighborhood" when we sneak in a late-April potluck/cookout on a Saturday night and start the planning at four o'clock in the afternoon. Thank God he has even one more place to be at home.

It is not just for safety that we live in our neighborhoods. It is also for fun. Unlocking our doors is simply a metaphor for unlocking our hearts so that they can have fun and mingle with other hearts.

I think about portals a lot. And thresholds. And how we go back and forth on them all day long. It is also nice to think about who can just walk in, without knocking. Who can use our portal? Our neighbors. Whose portal can we use? Our neighbors'. If we are all accustomed to walking back and forth, there will be much less silence and isolation and loneliness for a criminal to invade.

We must take back our days and our nights, our streets and our living rooms, our backyards and our neighborhoods. Then whether we lock or unlock, open or close, will matter much, much less than it does right now. It will matter in a proper way, at appropriate times, not inappropriate times. Women with small children won't need to be scared on cold nights; old people will find satisfaction in giving directions to neighbors they know. Kitty Genovese will be a name with no future, only a horrifying past.

We will all live post–Post Fear.

why unlock doors

Chapter 6
why spend more time at home

IF PAUL HAWKEN (OF THE SMITH AND HAWKEN GARDENING CATALOG) CAN REGRET HIS INVOLVEMENT WITH MAIL-ORDER SHOPPING, THEN I, AS A CARD-CARRYING FEMINIST, CAN REGRET MY INVOLVEMENT IN THE DEVELOPMENT OF THE TWO-CAREER FAMILY. I USED TO THINK IT WAS A GOOD IDEA. I NO LONGER DO.

Snow days convinced me. Once the machine of Mom to work, Dad to work, and kids to school gets going, it is very hard to turn its engine off. And my family is not alone in needing its engine turned off every now and then. Also, we are not a machine.

When things got to the point in our family where only the children could enjoy a snow day—and both adults flipped at the very possibility—we knew it was time for a change. We all—our children call us "stressed out" to our faces—knew we were working too hard. And we also knew that most of our friends were working too hard—making appointments for dinner dates two months in advance was one clue.

At first I thought it was simply an impossible and socially prohibited thought—that we could go forward to living on less money and less status than two salaries provided us. Going "back" to a one-career family was impossible; we had caught the bug of gender justice, and it is incurable. What was not impossible was imagining a less plugged-in life. A less rapid pace. A less harried existence. That was actually full of pleasure. The relationship of the two

salaries to peace was a better ratio than the frequency of our lovemaking to the week. The more salaries and status, the less peace. We were spending way too much of our time gaining the capacity to spend.

Everyone knows the figures. That Americans have less leisure time now than their parents did. That "rush" is our middle name. But few of us are acknowledging the relationship of the two-career family to the messy buildup of family anxiety. Even fewer are willing to name the complicity of feminism in the change.

Are feminists at fault? Of course not. Could we have been more in charge of the massive economic shift that happened while we were becoming free—a shift that meant women *had* to work outside the home as well as *wanting* to do so? I don't know how. It's not like we were in the driver's seat as the decisions were made about a changing economy.

Nevertheless, we may follow a pattern of thought. In the great words of Malcolm X, "Racism is not our fault but it is our responsibility." The anxiety of the current economy for the two-career family is not the fault of feminists, but it is our responsibility. We now have a voice in economic decisions. We are there in the workplace. We need to bring our values with us.

What do we need? Both men and women who are partners now in the madness of raising children and raising money. More snow days. Off time. Fun time. Time when we are prohibited or prohibit ourselves from running about. How do we get it? By roping and taming our economic appetites. By roping and taming the political economy and the housing economy. By rejoicing if and as housing prices fall, so that two incomes aren't needed for one house. By having flex-time, job sharing, and part-time jobs with benefits. By permitting ourselves the goodness of our desire for peace. Can we make these massive economic and value shifts by ourselves? Of course not. Can we make them together? Of course.

When the snow started to fall last week, it was clear that snow days were not far away. The first day off from school for the kids, my husband and I raced them to the sledding hill, jumped on the used toboggan we had picked up at a summer yard sale, and rode down the hill. The sled didn't steer and so we headed straight for the bump the other children had built. Over it went our aging backs. Ouch. When we realized we weren't dead, we had a good laugh. We were grateful for our vertebrae at the moment—but also scared. We know what an inability to work, even for a few days, would do to our professional lives. We'd get money, but we'd also get "behind." This one snow day was already causing that modern complaint known as desk stress to rage inside us.

But that first snow day took some of the anxiety away. Once we learned how to avoid the bump, all five of us were pretty good at the hill. The second snow day we found another spot, right in our own backyard, where the slope had a nice downhill grade. That night right after supper, when usually both of us had started what I call the circus—otherwise known as bedtime, replete with last-minute phone calls in and out, the dishes, the homework, the music, and the mess—my husband went outside and grabbed the toboggan. It took us about five minutes to put on the average of five wet garments each and get out the door. As we slid up and down the dark hill until way past bedtime, I was deeply glad. Something in my life was going rapidly downhill, not rapidly uphill. I was having fun. I had found some freedom from my economic orders, so richly obeyed by my own spiritual and political complicity. So had my family.

The increase of snow days would be a great national economic policy. And if it doesn't develop, I will gladly become more of a civil and cultural disobedient. If Paul Hawken can see that the very thing which made his life profitable—mail-order shopping—carried some problems with it, so can I. He recognizes that he helps people speed up their lives, then sells products that suggest that everything is slow and easy. His gardening catalogs and lifestyle objects are mythological more than practical. Both of us have helped life speed up. The two-career family is a big engine, going nowhere fast. One of the places I want to get to is the country of fun—and I don't know if I can get there from here. Thank God for snow days. May their numbers increase.

I think a lot about Marcia Clark, the lead prosecuting attorney in the O. J. Simpson trial. With every woman, she danced the jig of motherhood and work. But every woman doesn't have to do it in public view while also being threatened with a custody battle.

Because of her double bind, she showed us a lot about the two-career family that we feminists may not want to see. She showed us that husbands also need partners in raising children. If Clark's strung-out partner had been female, we would find the feminist choir out in force. Because he is a man, we feminists don't really take his explanations that seriously. Of course he should help with the children, the brute.

Clark's experience is a short course in the two-career family, and the final paper has yet to be written. Is it really possible for women—or men for that matter—to bear serious public responsibility with small children in the home? In the opening years of the cultural economy of two working parents, we all said yes to that question. We could share the home front and share the public world. We would give our children quality time.

Now that quality time is even discredited as a cliché—everyone knows children don't want *quality* time, they want *quantity* time—we have had to wonder why our money doesn't stretch so far. One reason is we had to provide quantity-time care and pay nannies. It is not an accident in this early period of two parents working outside the home that nanny taxes are an Achilles' heel for many otherwise honest people.

To reiterate: Children don't want quality time so much as they want someone sitting right there when they happen to scrape their knees. That may take hours. But children want presence, not crash landings, in their lives. They want accompaniment.

They are dull partners 95 percent of the time. When they do ask for Mom or Dad to "watch," they want that person to have been waiting for the invitation. Not that stay-at-home mothers were that much better at paying acute attention at previously unannounced times. But now, with the children's market share of time being an hour or so a day, it is very hard for them to schedule their drama.

Marcia Clark is obviously a good attorney. She wouldn't have argued what she argued otherwise. But her pain, her fence, her situation was an exemplary contemporary tragedy. Women are tragic actors in the current world: damned if we do and damned if we don't. Either we excel at two things that are impossible to excel at simultaneously or we have done something that culture and economy think of as wrong. In this kind of a box, it is hard *not* to hurt our children with our own anxiety.

The two-career family is a social, economic, and spiritual disaster of serious proportion for both men and women. Men want quantity time too. Men want company. So do women. We all want someone special to watch over us, not just for our scraped knee, but for our other hurts and our other joys as well.

At the sixth-grade orientation for junior high school here, held last week at seven o'clock on a Monday evening, most of the children were home cooking their own suppers. The parents came, but the children did not. Our children are raising themselves.

Two-career couples are caught on a fence. They need the second salary, but each partner also needs much more from the other than what they are now getting. Nobody is winning in the two-career family—and yet no one seems to be willing to write the final paper. We seem, rather, stuck—knowing that we can't live with it but also not being able to imagine how we could live without it. Simultaneously with the feminist thrust into public life, the economy changed. The rent went up. Now both of us are needed behind the middle-class plow.

Marcia Clark, what will you do next? Your answer is our answer. Then again, maybe those of us who are free from the spotlight need to be the ones who experiment with alternatives. Poverty is clearly one. Getting hold of the "new" employment age, and doubling the salary of one worker in cyberspace is another. Apparently one person can now do the work of two. Will he/she be paid double?

Flex-time, the return of the extended family under one roof, guaranteed income during child-raising years, seriously good child care, job sharing—round up the usual suspects, and we may yet have a pro-family economic policy. But don't let anybody think Clark was not the mother of the year. We all know what she was up against. Don't let anybody not sympathize with her spouse. We see what he is up against also. With the ancient text of Exodus 20:12, we beg society to honor our fathers and our mothers.

The way we have managed in our household is to have a nanny/sister/aunt/friend, whose name is Nancy. Nancy came to live with us when our children were young, and she is still here. She first shared a bedroom with Katie, then we moved into a house with a separate but attached apartment. She moved with us from New York to Massachusetts. She is the only one who can really remember to pick up the milk. She is the best cardplayer in the place. She is also the least active in economic terms, but does have her own job, car, and bills. Three adults for three children? We begin to get close to taking care of them this way.

And, God knows, there are plenty of unattached people who would like to attach. We happened on our solution by accident. Now that the kids are older, and Nancy is ready to move on to a more independent life (nuclear family living when you're not part of a nuclear family is not all pleasure), we thank God that we got lucky. I wonder what it will take for society to get lucky.

Write Letters Why

Why We: 10 Wa

ays to Simplify —

10 Ways and

Enjoy & Your Li

Chapter 7
why use the branch library

EVEN IF THE SOUTH AMHERST LIBRARY DID NOT HAVE A PLEASANT LIBRARIAN WHO KNOWS MOST CLIENTS BY NAME, AND EVEN IF IT DID NOT SIT IN A RIGHT-SIZED BUILDING ON A RIGHT-SIZED COMMON, AND EVEN IF IT DID NOT HAVE THE AURA OF HOMEY MESS, IT WOULD STILL BE WORTH USING.

The reasons are many. The branch library keeps you out of the center of things. It lets you enjoy the edges. Centralization is an offense to branching. Branching is what makes trees interesting, what makes communities interesting, and what causes character in a town. My real estate values depend on the character of this community. There is enough threatening that character already: hamburger and pizza joints that creep across town in the same way that raspberries used to march across lawns. Creeping homogenization and creeping franchization. With so many other threats to our local character already, we may as well enjoy all that we have left.

In addition to the assault on local character, there is the matter of children's memories. We don't want everything they remember in later years to be franchised. We want the children of South Amherst to remember cold winter afternoons when they sat in small, book-smelling rooms, reading a story about a girl who escaped from modern life. She wandered beyond McDonald's, beyond the Main Reading Room, beyond Gap, off the well-beaten Robert Frost trail. Her memory had something no one else's memory could have had. The room in which she had the now-remembered experience was the right size for a child's memory.

Of course, she could have such individualization in the central library in town. It too has enough magic to light lamps along the streams of children's unconscious memories. But the branches here and elsewhere have child-size magic. One good lamp is worth a lot, for a long time.

When towns get too cheap to support oddball things—as branch libraries are nowadays when I can access the whole megillah by pushing five more buttons—we say goodbye to a history that isn't dead yet.

If you have ever taken the long way, the back road, the "discovered" road, you know exactly what I mean. It is an adventure to get to where you are going but to go another way. There is real virtue in the oddball route. Ask anybody who has taken a vacation and had the added pleasure of finding an out-of-the-way place. Communities need out-of-the-way places. Branch libraries are just that.

They are places we can go when we have nowhere else to go. They have chairs to sit in that are public and private at the same time. They offer our vacant afternoons a welcome, even if we don't have any vacant afternoons. We can imagine that some day we might and then we can imagine our-selves sitting in their chairs.

If someone knew our name when we walked in, even better. But that is not the essential point. The essential point is protecting the nooks and crannies of communities—the way good interior decorators recommend many different kinds of chairs in a house, or window seats, or maximizing the garrets and cupolas and minimizing the ticky-tacky, where everything looks the same.

Resisting homogenization has become a matter of great expense in a world that confuses value with cost. Of course, it seems cheaper to centralize. But it isn't. It just costs less money. But there are other ways to pay besides in cash. Remember whole-cost accounting? It shows that losing small libraries is very expensive. The cost is character, children's memories, old roads. The cost is the loss of the odd-ball, the unusual, the right size.

What I love most about libraries is sitting in them. I know why—because it reminds me of my childhood when I was free at an early age to roam the streets of Kingston, New York, and end up at the tiny public library. There I read every book in the place. It gave my early life a sense of completeness. I probably read lots of books I didn't even like. (Now I find myself saying that a novel is too long. Too long for what? For my investment in it. The novel is probably not too long—my life has become too short, especially if I can't take the time to read.)

Nathaniel Hawthorne said that "happiness is a butterfly, which when pursued, is always just beyond your grasp, but which if you will sit down quietly, may alight upon you." Many people have lost their ability to sit down quietly. Public libraries, especially the smaller ones, welcome us. They invite us to sit down in a place that feels as good as our own living room but is larger than that. It is the community living room. Anything can happen when we are sitting and calm. Happiness may even come along.

I remember in college that we tested more than one limit. The class of 1969 wore odd clothes, used odd speech, read weird books. One day, my most conservative friend, who later endowed the college library significantly from his wealth, tested the library's dress code. He wore Bermuda shorts in and through the main entrance. He was greeted by the college librarian herself, one Mrs. Smoke, with these words: "Mr. Hobor, we are not a beach." She loved libraries so much that she felt one should dress properly to enter them. While I wouldn't go that far today, I admit I do find libraries elegant, no matter how delightfully dowdy chairs and fixtures have become in these days of budget cutbacks. Libraries are the emblems of quality in a world that has forgotten the word.

It is not an accident that our family's favorite musical is *The Music Man*, in which an Iowa librarian and a charlatan fall in love. Their community also learns how to make music. It is the collaboration of her classic sturdiness and his classic phoniness that constitutes the faith of the story. The children make music because they think they can, not because they can. At one point the Irish mother of the spinster librarian, Marian, makes fun of her daughter's "library full of booooks," as though that could get her somewhere in life. The reason we love Marian and her strangely titled love story is that Marian would be just fine with her library full of booooks. She loves them. They love her. And she knows when to put them down, and when to hide them from the mayor as well. Marian is as much a librarian as a pigeon or poodle is Parisian. She embodies libraries. She loves them, lives them, and knows when to turn their wisdom toward another goal, that of romantic love or a child's music. It is by faking knowledge from a book that she gains her liberation from the library she loves so well.

We bought our house in Amherst from the man who for many years was the editor of the *New York Times Book Review*. He had inherited the house from his father, a chicken farmer. Here we raise chickens and read books, among other things. The delight of the house is that it has bookshelves everywhere. In every nook and cranny, shelves have been built.

Thus a friend referred to the house as decorated in the "early library" style. We could not have been more pleased.

Right down the street is the branch library, less than a mile away. It snuggles into the South Amherst common, maintaining a safe distance from the South Congregational Church, its parsonage, and its orchard. When they are all closed or dormant, the library is still open. Three nights a week, most afternoons. Through it you can access the main collections of the local university, college, and bigger libraries. Through it you can get to the world. Because of it, we don't have to fill up all of Mr. Brown's shelves.

Henry David Thoreau swore he could travel the whole world in Concord. We can too. From just one branch.

why use the branch library

Write Letters Why

Why Wri10 Wa

ays to Simplify —

10 Ways and

Enjoy & Your Lif

and S

Chapter 8
why take trains

THERE ARE SO MANY WAYS TO GET PLACES THAT THEY CAN HARDLY BE COUNTED. WE CAN WALK. WE CAN DRIVE. WE CAN TAKE A BUS OR TRAIN. WE CAN FLY. WE CAN SLED. WE CAN TAKE THE BACK ROAD OR THE NEW ROAD, THE LONG WAY OR THE SHORT WAY. ON MY WAY TO WORK THE SHORT ROUTE MISSES THE WATERFALL. THE LONG WAY INCLUDES IT. I LOVE TO GO THE LONG WAY—AND NOT JUST FOR THE WATERFALL BUT ALSO FOR THE SENSE OF FREEDOM I HAVE WHEN I DON'T LET SPEED BE MY ONLY CRITERION FOR LIVING.

If you've ever watched the opening rituals of a family gathering, you know how much people love talking about ways to get places. The men will almost always begin to discuss routes. "I took Route 9 and it took me forty-five minutes from the diner." . . . "I took the pike but missed the . . ." And on and on.

My less-than-utopian job requires me to cover four counties and to drive every day. I have found ways to love even the terror and tyranny of my car, like placing little photos on the dash for meditation. The spring my aunt died I kept her picture there for a month. It let me say goodbye to her. Car tapes have allowed me to "read" the best novels of my life and to enjoy Gregorian chants, gospel music, and Mozart. Every Sunday a Bach cantata carries me on my way to a distant church. And I sing out loud and talk to myself. Cars, especially their privacy and freedom, can be fun.

Driving cars connects us to one another in more ways than we can even imagine. It ratifies our decision on behalf of speed. We drive because it takes us "there" quicker. Driving confirms our value of freedom. "I would carpool," some say, "but then I lose my freedom during the day." Driving forms the infrastructure of our life—not just the highways, but also the economy of oil and gas and steel. Not just now, but later: the hole in the ozone will affect our lives just as the whole of the ozone used to protect our lives. The hole comes from cars, from daily freedom and speed.

No one has to repeat the politically correct argument against cars. It has been made so often that you probably skimmed the last paragraph. What we need is the positive argument: how to get places without cars.

I personally would prefer a world where normal movement was by train. Trains are more fun than cars. They have romance. When they pull out of the station, you have enough time to know you're on your way. Their start-up is gracious. And in some ways they are a world unto themselves. As my daughter put it once while we were checking in to our roomette on a night train to Chicago—just hear it, a night train to Chicago—"We have everything we need, right here." She was referring to the toothbrush holder.

Trains are communal in an all-American way; they retain your freedom, so you don't *have* to commune, but *may.* I have met some great friends in the piano car of the Montrealer. When my divorce was final over a decade ago, I knew I had to do something to ritualize the end of a youthful marriage. I couldn't think of a thing. But then I found myself on a train from New Haven to New York, onto the Montrealer, overnight, and checking into a hotel in Montreal in the morning. There I took a bubble bath and got back on the next train to New York. When White River Junction appeared out the window on the way back, I jumped off the train. There was an aimlessness about the travel, something that automobiles can reproduce—but only with your direction. I liked being directed for a change.

The night trains to Cleveland and to Chicago get plenty of use by me because of the location of our denomination's offices in the Midwest. I can leave home at 7 P.M. and wake up in Cleveland at 7:45 A.M., have a day of meetings, then get back on the train at 3 A.M. and be home by 1 P.M. the next day. Many call this a ridiculous waste of time. They don't know how quiet a train is, how good the rivers look, how interesting the back ends of old American cities are. How the phone doesn't ring. How refreshing it is to know that every place doesn't look the same.

When I fly, I get there too soon. I get confused about where I am, especially in airports that are frighteningly much the same.

Trains make sense for work-related travel because they allow time to think, to plan, to dream, and to be uninterrupted. A lot of people would call that time off. I don't.

Train travel makes even more sense for fun than it does for business. It is much cheaper than flying or driving, and it gives glimpses of the country that used to be. We all travel to get away from the normal—and our daily landscape is a piece of the normal we need to get away from. Enough malls. Trains take us through old towns and cities in such a way that you can still see the old shape.

The old landscape. Before we high-rised and sky-scraped it.

Traveling with children in this way is an almost necessary part of their education. Take a child on a cross-country trip. Amtrak charges full price for adults, half for children, with "fly back" options available for the time deprived. The trip, including all meals and a room, costs about five hundred dollars for an adult and takes four days.

I have taken each one of my children at least one way across. My train habit started when I realized I could fly by myself or ride with one of them for the same money. Since I often had speaking engagements in different parts of the country, my costs were subsidized.

When my daughter Katie, then six, and I went to Seattle one May, we saw a bear eat a salmon on an island in the Columbia River. We used an African mouth harp to lull each other to sleep each night. Katie made good friends with another girl on the train. Her mother and I made a child care arrangement. She took mornings to listen to their animated imagination games, and I took afternoons.

Knowing that Isaac has seen Albuquerque, that Jacob has seen Virginia foothills and Katie has seen the Rockies, and that I have seen them each see the great American land gives me a great gladness. I know that some of what they see is what Americans want to forget, the old country, the old ways. But I don't want to forget. I want to remember just how beautiful it is.

I took the last trip of the Montrealer—now the Vermonter because its route has been shrunk—just to make sure I would not forget it. It last pulled out of the station on March 31, 1995.

Before the Montrealer was junked, it would pull into the Amherst station about 2 A.M. daily. The train took up all the space there is on Main and Railroad streets. It curved out of Amherst College going north with a graceful propriety. Track bent to train as though a good tailor had handmade the suit. The noise was equally filling. Night silence yielded to the complete sound of the great engine.

Even now with the day train coming in and going only to Vermont, I am not just another van-driving parent in the line at Crocker Farm School dropping off the kids in my concealed flannel night-gown. When the conductor in the wink of an eye dismounts the train and calls, "All aboard," he means me. I am a part of the "all." I am about to be aboard.

The quiet of the train ride is broken by snoring men and snuggling babies. Young men dance in their seats to rock and roll piped to their ears only. On the last night of the old Montrealer run, I sat down next to an older woman who got off at Montpelier later that morning for her mother's funeral. She had a hand-crocheted blanket on her lap. When I sat down, she moved her vinyl purse to the other side of her seat, nodded at me, and returned to sleep. We didn't talk till the breakfast that we shared. She had brought two rolls with her. I got the coffee.

What is great about the train is the way it is not the plane. It is blue-collar, not white-collar, transportation. When the mayors of the Northeast met to defend the Montrealer against the great ax from Atlanta, they were defending the blue collars. The vinyl purses. The woman with three children who somehow manages to let them all sleep on her all night. These people were the Montrealer's constituency. Someone had to remind the so-tight-they-squeak crowd about the needs of the un-rich for transportation. When their mother dies, they go to the funeral on the train. They can't afford the plane. They bring their own breakfast.

Thank God for the mayors. They were not defending my romancing of the rail. They were defending the people who still don't have dependable cars. The cars of Amtrak's passengers long ago lost their ability to go out of town. Those tires are bald, the spark plugs long past consistent spark. Train people are different from plane people. The difference is economic class. As Thomas Wolfe puts it so well in his great novel about New York, some people are subway people. Others take cabs.

I am sure it took a while for the mayors to get around to the working poor. Surely they have plenty to do. Reforming welfare is not a part-time job. Nor is governing while government has become the national enemy of choice, the new "Communist." When you have to defend Big Bird and Beethoven in the same week you have to defend the poor, you hardly have any time for the train. Thank God they saw the privatizing ax coming toward the train and at least said something.

The Vermonter, a small imitation of the Montrealer, has one year to "prove itself" and then Vermont will withdraw its funding. The criterion of beauty or fun or the utility to the poor will probably not be the criterion by which it will have to be proven.

Perhaps trains could be run privately just as well as they are run publicly. The Montrealer was rarely on time. It did away with its piano bar in the late seventies—the epitome of bureaucratic stupidity if anything is. The food service on the trains is clearly run by a committee. Not that the food is bad, but there are more rules about how it should be ordered and eaten than there are train charges on my lifetime Visa card.

In addition to my cross-country credentials and my Montrealer repetition, I also once got bumped off a train in Boise, Idaho, because I hurt my toe and they were afraid I'd sue if I wasn't medicated. All these trips, replete with adventures, are a form of recreation for me. They clear my mind of the residue of my leather purse.

Privatizing Amtrak might even help my habit for the train. It is surely not something that I fear. The trains are often full, even on the East Coast, where service has deteriorated pitiably. The maintenance is all west and south of Chicago: you can feel the difference in the tracks and the smooth of the ride immediately. People say it's Congress and pork. Without Congress and pork, the Montrealer could do just fine getting from here to there. If any more of our trains go the way of the now-silenced Montrealer, too much will be lost.

Anthony Trollope tells of a train trip to London to deliver a novel. The publisher hated it and insulted Trollope's work to his face. On the way home on the train, Trollope turned over the novel and began a new one on the back pages of the old.

Maybe we need the rewrite. Maybe we are about to get a new train service. And a new government. And a new welfare system. And a newly alert private system of corporations. Maybe. God knows some beast has been let out of the American cage and is slouching toward Bethlehem. Or Sodom. Or both. Any beast that thinks it can't afford beautiful music, trains, and the poor must be watched very carefully!

As long as a few mayors are around defending those who aren't rich enough to fly, perhaps the beast will warm up to its subjects. Perhaps it will learn how to say yes, as well as no. We may just be showing the courage of Trollope, turning the page over and beginning again. Or we may be just insulting each other, and music and trains and women with three children curled all around them. Whatever happens, I just want to be sure that the leather and vinyl purses can still have breakfast together on their way north, every now and then.

I want to ride on more than memories.

Chapter 9
why seek calm through courage

Mary McCarthy said that her friend Hannah Arendt was "a solitary passenger on her own train of thought." I wonder how I really feel about that comment, or her saying it about her friend. Still, I know what it means. There are moments in life when we are all alone. No one else can imagine why we are doing what we are doing, and we ourselves are less than sure.

We know we don't want to live by the marching orders of more, most, better, and quickest, but we don't know how to stop. There don't seem to be many alternatives. And so we live with a level of stress that is often unbearable. Rather than let each other know, we keep on keeping on. We smile when a grimace would be more appropriate. Who has the time for long and complex conversations about how difficult it really is?

I watched my friend stay solitary at a stress workshop our area was offering for clergy. She was so stressed out she had to leave the stress workshop early! We both found her departure hilarious. There wasn't much to do but laugh. She was starting a new job and has three children. I also have three children, so I understood her situation. I managed to stay for the workshop; it was so dull at times that I could catch up on some of my correspondence. This kind of two-timing often makes me glad; it is a modern form of beating the system.

I did buy the product the seminar was selling: biodots. The first day my tab stayed black—meaning "very stressed out"—all day. I desperately hoped for it to move to green (normal) or turquoise (relaxed) or even blue (calm). It did not. I determined to change my life, radically, as soon as a few more baskets of laundry were folded.

The few days I wore the black dots were a genuine threat to my existence. They told me that I was carrying way too much stress. And the more aware I became of how much stress I was carrying, the worse it became. You can't imagine my relief to discover that I needed the "cold hands" version of the product. Calm returned. My biodot turned green.

The calm I needed was already there, pulsing in the temperature of my blood. But I did not know it. And I knew I had enough trouble to warrant the black dot. I feel most days like I carry around two large suitcases of detail, without the benefit of a luggage carrier. The suitcases have to be moved in that time-honored way of carrying one forward, setting it down, then going back for the other, and so on. Even so, I don't like the definition of this baggage as stress. I like to put it down long enough, each day, to let the earth hold it so I can hold something else. I like to park it and leave it, and hope someone will steal it. What if someone steals it?

Once at the Fort Lauderdale airport my husband returned the rental car while I took the children, all three in diapers, to the gate. I assumed when he dropped us off at the United Airlines counter that he would surely take care of the luggage as well as the car. He assumed, at the same time, that I would surely take care of the luggage as well as the children. We both had justice on the side of our assumption. But neither of us took care of the luggage. We were both carrying enough. Imagine our surprise when we got to New York and waited for our luggage, which did not arrive. It was still in Florida. Fortunately, United picked it up for us and put it on the next plane. They had been wondering who left all that stuff there.

I love this story. It gives me deep calm. I don't want to get too mushy about United Airlines, but ever since that moment, I have had a deep trust in them. They were just what I needed—another set of hands, another something to help me carry what I have to carry.

Once I was driving along, late for yet another meeting, on the Massachusetts Turnpike. On the radio Ella Fitzgerald was crooning "Someone to Watch Over Me." I lost it. I had to pull off the road. My yearning for someone to watch over me was so intense that I couldn't imagine her singing about it, right there, in my van, on the turnpike. Stress? No. That is too minor a version of the problem.

I have actually hated the word *stress* since I first heard it. It has a bad hissing sound and doesn't adequately describe the issue. The issue is nerve. The issue is fear. The issue is calm.

The issue is best described by Nelson Mandela when David Frost asked him about his genuine hope for South Africa. One would imagine he would have a political or economic answer. He did not. He had a spiritual answer: "Freedom from fear." Mandela said that his hope for his country lay in the death of fear, the fear of oneself, the fear of the other, the fear of the unknown, the fear of the everyday circumstances of one's life.

I may have more stress than I dare admit. But I

would rather call it fear. I have fear. I am feared-out. If there was a measurement for fear, I am sure I would rank high.

When we are afraid, biodots tell us the bad news. When we are free from fear, we can relax. We can live the way we are meant to live: we can live calmly.

I first discovered the meaning of calm by being a mother. There are lots of other settings, at work, at the PTA, at the Little League play-offs, where calm has virtue. I simply learned most of what I know about calmness from parenting, although you don't have to have children to know its importance.

I always assumed that I'd be a courageous moth-er. My children would be fearlessly protected from junk food. Their bad teachers would be banned. Their earaches would always settle homeopathically. They would be better than their time and place, and I would be their shield, the guardian at the gate, allowing them to tunnel out of "here" into "there." Whenever they would say, "Everyone else does it," or "has" it, I would stand peerless—I mean fearless.

I wanted more calm than courage. Then I dis-covered that the route to courage, these days, is calm. Our home has been colonized by culture. My children are not only not pure: they are not even close to pure. Tainted is what they are. It started with *Sesame Street* and *Mister Rogers* and soon became TV time at 5 P.M. From whole-wheat crust we moved rapidly to memorizing the local Domino's Pizza number. Any books now replaced good books. And all these invasions happened before the children even reached public school.

The trip from guardian parent to conquered territory took a few brief years. I had neither the time nor the energy for my courageous principles. Thank God.

I was not cut out to be a fundamentalist parent. Instead of the perfection I wanted, I remained calm. When the kids turned the French bread into the guns I wouldn't let them have, I neither blessed nor cursed their behavior. Instead, I observed. I made sure they knew that I knew what they were doing. "Please don't kill each other," I would say quietly. When my daughter refused any clothing that was not pink, I also refused critical commentary. This, too, I assured myself, would pass. It did.

The first time my ten-year-old cursed, I put him in his room, closed his door, and didn't let him out for one hour. All without showing my tears of shame and rage. Was my lack of exposure right or wrong, courageous or cowardly? Calmly, I don't know. I no longer expect myself to know. I know and love my children well enough to know that they need me *beside* them, not in front protecting them. The protection of the fundamentalist came with too high a price tag: I was much too right, culture much too wrong. Fundamentalism of any variety hurts children.

Yes, I do require religious education for them. And milk. And vegetables. Beyond that I am too wishy-washy to be courageous. Too "in" the world to be above it. Too much of a follower of my children, wanting to go with them where they go and not to be left behind in a past that wasn't nearly as perfect as I imagined it to be.

When Katie broke her arm trying to climb a rope, I actually drove the van to the hospital in twenty minutes without passing out. I did not stare at the broken bone poking out of her left wrist. I did not let her see me cry. The doctor made me leave the room when he set the bone. Katie screamed for me not to go. I referred her to her own inner strength. She said she didn't have any. I assured her she did and left the room. Later I asked her how her inner strength had served her in the clinch. She beamed. "Just fine, Mom, just fine."

Isaac broke his foot as he was sliding into home plate. He was in the first month of his best Little League season yet, at the top of his game, pitching, catching, and hitting. He cried so much in the emergency room about the loss of baseball that he forgot how much his foot hurt. The nurses all cried; even the doctor got misty. There wasn't a thing I could do.

Calm can't control, but it remains a worthy destination nonetheless. Calm, through courage, is my destination as a parent. Partnership is my hope more than leadership. I can't control all that I had hoped to control. Whenever I try, the biodot dot turns black. When I stop trying to control things, my dot turns to its calmer colors. I become sufficiently free of fear to be calm.

No, I am not Zen-parenting yet. Hardly. I still wear the dots every now and then just to see how I am doing. But just like my courage, I have to learn to keep those dots in their place.

One of the biggest enemies to calm is each other. We can help each other, but mostly we hurt.

Sometimes I think that adding to the stress of modern life is the self-protective coverup we have going on. We may actually compete with each other not to show our stress as much as the Joneses do.

Watergate had its Deep Throat, and most of us have a closet full of costumes and masks. We don't always want to tell all that we know, about ourselves or each other. Among women, and those men who are also signed up for the two-career rat race, there is enough stress/fear or fear/stress to sink a ship. But we don't like to admit it to each other. It is a form of cowardice, a breaking of line, a failure to report for duty. And so we ride our solitary train of thought. We laugh when our friends leave the stress workshop early. We are not capable of doing much else.

We may not need to have long conversations every day about how tough it is, but every now and then a good long one is necessary. In that discussion, we may tell the truth about just how black the biodot gets some days. We can take our own solitary train of thought out of its station. We can lose our luggage. We can let our Deep Calm tell its truth.

Why not? What do we have to lose? The fiction that we are coping with everything just fine, thank you. The fiction that we are in charge. The fiction that we are fearless, when you'd have to be stupid not to be afraid. One older man put it quite well when he described his aging years as a time when a "mild depression would only make good sense."

If you're raising a family today and you're not afraid, you don't see what is happening. That's why calm is so essential: it acknowledges fear. It doesn't say it is not afraid. Rather, it admits it is afraid—but it also lives more deeply, in the residence of calm.

What is there to fear? That our children will have even tougher, lower-paying jobs than we have. That the ozone will not hold. That even more people will be more poor. That we will not raise our children with enough inner resources and their biodots will all turn black. That French cheese will be taken off the menu.

Under the circumstances, we need all the stress workshops we can get. All the Mandelas we can find. All the calm we can muster. All the friends we already have and a few more. Hannah Arendt may have been traveling on her own solitary train of thought—but thank God, Mary McCarthy knew that's where she was.

why seek calm through courage

Chapter 10

EVERY SABBATH IS A LITTLE EASTER, A LITTLE TIME UNPLUGGED, RATHER THAN PLUGGED IN. IT DOESN'T HAVE TO BE SUNDAY, OR SATURDAY EITHER. WE CAN UNPLUG EVEN MORE FREQUENTLY IF WE WANT. BUT IT IS DANGEROUS TO THE HUMAN SOUL TO UNPLUG LESS OFTEN THAN WEEKLY. WE BURN OUT OUR MOTORS. WE THINK OF TIME AS ONLY NOW, AND WE FORGET ITS LARGER DIMENSIONS.

In Sabbath time, we have time off rather than being on time or having time be on us. Sabbath means holy rest. It means separation, the separation of work life from the rest of life. People used to think that life on these rotations was normal; now we just yearn for rest, holy or not, with an anxious vigor. "I need to get away." "Stop the merry-go-round; I want to get off." People say these things but don't do much about them—until we make a habit out of Sabbath.

Worshiping every Sunday—or fasting every Saturday, or climbing a mountain every Tuesday—is a way of keeping Sabbath. Of keeping the Third Commandment, of remembering the Sabbath day to keep it holy. As a religious pursuit, it is the most pragmatic. People who separate time, who take time off, do better in their time on. So many sociological studies prove this that one would think more bosses would pay attention to the facts. At least one large employer does: McDonald's asks its employees to meditate for at least one hour a day, on the job.

If you have ever practiced meditation, you know why McDonald's is doing so well: Impossible problems turn solvable after an hour away from them. In the Sabbath of meditation, we make all of our day holy, not just part of it. We go back refreshed—and eventually understand life as less back and off and more as a full fabric that includes time at rest and time at work. Precisely by separating time into different uses, we unify it.

I realize that some people haven't had a Sabbath for a long time. I can see it in their eyes and hear it in their speech. I recognize the Sabbathlessness easily: I go through periods of time quite frequently when I can't imagine that I have time to rest. I know the frightened-deer look of getting through another family dinner, evening meeting, and children's baths—with the dishes and laundry waiting at a time I might prefer to turn into a blob and watch the news. I know the speech of *can't, late, not enough,* and *impossible* very well.

The contents of the nightly news make their own argument on behalf of the Sabbath—and thereby intensify the stupidity of not resting. How can we possibly manage the blues of the news without our full selves? And how can we have our full selves if we don't rest them? The news tells us of floods, fires, and earthquakes, along with murders and other forms of violence. It issues a nightly warning that we should write our calendars in pencil.

Not only have many people not had a Sabbath for a long time—from either their own laundry or the nightly news—some have gone a long time without an Easter, even though the date has come and gone. By Easter I mean resurrection. Raised up. Lifted above. That Sabbath which is larger than even weekly rest. That movement into another room from which things seem possible rather than impossible.

William Blake said that death is moving into another room. He was right. And resurrection is the same. We stop living with the furniture of cynicism, the paintings of realism, the rugs of dust, dreary colors, worn spots, the windows painted shut. We begin living in a room where the windows are wide open, the bright colors shifting with the light that flows in. We live as though our hopes were real—that universal health insurance is not a series of interacting impossibilities but a normal, manageable, reasonable way to live, given the reality of sickness. That the children now without either Easter breakfast or any breakfast will soon be served, right here in this new room. That life is as spicy and aromatic as the herbs used to wash the body of Jesus. That we ourselves will do what we can of what we must—that we will find ourselves with clean, folded clothes—and a good spir-

it of good humor in even our latest and longest meetings. And barring that, we will be able to imagine a change in the weather and work by next week.

In the uplift of Easter and Sabbath, instead of being called "aging," we think of ourselves as just beginning. Instead of being old hippies, we manage a little wiggle in our walk (sexual harassment notwithstanding). Not that Easter is permanent youth, but rather that youth is permanent—if not for us, for someone. If not for us, for the earth. If not for the earth, then for rock and roll, Gershwin, the Montrealer, and dark green lettuce.

In the uplift of Easter and Sabbath, we are able not only to manage the fact that many children in

Sarajevo have lost their hope, but also we remember that we saw a few of them sledding in the snow of the February cease-fire. Hope or no hope.

We also fake hope with less guilt, once holy rest is a room in our house. I know a man named Jerry who said that he never thought he would really die from AIDS: "I will live by that magic hope that being good will save me." I wish his room were bigger but it's not. At least he has some magic in it.

Sabbath rest is more than magic. It is more than a facelift where, as one writer has put it, "the past is erased at the expense of character." Easter is confidence about character. It is confidence about the other rooms. It is an acknowledgment that more is going on than meets the eye. It is the art of building the airplane while flying. It is resting while going flat out. Letting Sabbath be a part of our Monday as well as our Sunday attitude. A coffee break, as it were, where we do nothing else but drink the coffee.

Easter Sabbath even has a little institutional hope about it. Most people are in the tongue-clicking stage about institutional religion. Ain't it awful, they say. How could I trust my most delicate hopes in either the afterlife or life this afternoon in an institution as absurd as the church? I may be willing to take a Sabbath but I can't possibly take it with other people, on Sunday mornings or Friday nights. If we are going to give ourselves the permission to rest, we want to do it with the upper crust. Nature. A good brunch.

But Sabbath, over time, allows us to mix with those we may consider religious hypocrites. It is the holy break with ordinary time that matters—not whom we do it with. Religious people for centuries have marked time by Friday evenings or Sunday mornings, by forty days in Advent or Lent or Ramadan. These decisions are not dumb or bourgeois. They show the genuine wisdom of ordinary people. Before we give up on the institutional religions as a disciplined way to keep Sabbath, we had best check in with our snob factor. It exists inside the churches and temples as hypocrisy—and outside the churches and temples as the presumption that some of us are above hypocrisy.

Once we live in the other room of Easter, we understand that what we have viewed as the absurdity of religious institutions is precisely what we may and must trust. Proof of the resurrection, proof of the uplift, is not going to come. We will have to live by something other than proof. By something other than a perfect community of partnership in Sabbath keeping. We will have to live by the grace that comes through the rest of Sabbath.

Then we become the kind of people who can tolerate the absurdity of organized religion. The fact that many "religious" people are an unholy joke tells us that hypocrisy is never far from any door. And that we may, nevertheless, be glad of life. And imagine ourselves as truthful people.

William Sloane Coffin probably described Easter best in now-antiquated jargon: "I'm not o.k., and you're not o.k., and that's o.k." Who knows what can possibly happen between now and the next time we know Easter, the next time we know a Sabbath rest? Lots. The news will fill up again tonight. So will our calendars, our minds, and our hearts. The more that happens, the more Sabbath we need to digest it.

If we pay more attention to the orientation of our hearts than to the turning of the calendar's pages, we will find a little worship. We can count on the uplift of keeping Sabbath. On life being beautiful even when it does not seem so. We need to have one room that is kept distinct from the others. We need from its base to redecorate our other rooms. Frankly, you could argue that the whole place needs a new interior design. Sabbath provides that on a regular basis.

Parts of even the old mainline churches are already living in the new room. Women are welcomed in leadership positions; congregations are key antidotes to the individualism of society; heart-led spirituality is replacing the old head-led stuff. If we need partners to keep Sabbath, we need to look no further than down the street, on the corner. But if we can't tolerate partners that already have buildings, we can use our own houses and our own friends. Keeping Sabbath is the important thing—mostly for us, but also for all that we love.

Sabbath reminds us that we are not supposed to be in charge all the time. Only some of the time. It reminds us that some people are very hypocritical—and that they are still people. Just like us. Rather *too* much like us, if the truth be told. Keeping Sabbath helps us to remember who we are. And who we want to be. And why we were made. For rest and work, work and rest, both, not either. In keeping Sabbath, we make separations precisely to experience the deeper unities.

Why keep Sabbath? As a form of spiritual judo, it is unparalleled. It is rest tossed at work. It is roaming tossed at rushing. It is slow tossed at fast. Sabbath is the time in which we must write a letter and the time in which we may write a letter. It is an island of calm after a mainland of courage, all week long. It is time to remember how strong we have been "out there," how much we accomplished, not how much is left to do. Sabbath is song, and trains, and dancing, and unlocked doors. It is watching lettuce grow. It is the time after we have kept house to enjoy it. Sabbath is time to get lost in a good book.

Sabbath is a letter we write about ourselves, just to make sure we remember who we are.